SEASONS

in

THYME

FAVORITE RECIPES & MENUS

from the

JUNIOR LEAGUE OF BIRMINGHAM,

MICHIGAN, INC.

SEASONS
in
THYME

FAVORITE RECIPES & MENUS

from the

JUNIOR LEAGUE OF BIRMINGHAM,

MICHIGAN, INC.

SEASONS *in* THYME

FAVORITE RECIPES & MENUS
from the
JUNIOR LEAGUE OF BIRMINGHAM, MICHIGAN, INC.

Published by the Junior League of Birmingham, Michigan, Inc.

© 2003 Junior League of Birmingham, Michigan, Inc.

Junior League of Birmingham, Michigan
248-646-2613
jlbinc@htdconnect.com

This cookbook is a collection of favorite recipes, which are not necessarily original recipes.

Library of Congress Catalog Number: 2002106814

ISBN: 0-9720369-0-3

Edited, Designed, and Manufactured by
Favorite Recipes® Press
An imprint of

FRP

P.O. Box 305142
Nashville, Tennessee 37230
800-358-0560

Art Director: Steve Newman
Book Design: David Malone
Editor: Judy Jackson

Manufactured in the United States of America
First Printing: 2003
10,000 copies

COOKBOOK COMMITTEE

CO-CHAIRS
Colette O'Connor   Amy Risius

RECIPE COORDINATOR
Jennifer Soley

NON-RECIPE TEXT
Nancy Carabio Belanger

TREASURER
Angie Schmucker

COMMITTEE

Karen Anderson	Melissa Barrett	Jennifer Dix
Cathy Armstrong	Wendy Cummins	Bonnie Reed
Jennifer Ballarin	Renee Delsignore	Barbara Velasco

MISSION STATEMENT

The Junior League of Birmingham, Michigan, Incorporated, is an organization
of women committed to promoting voluntarism, developing the potential of
women, and improving the community through effective action and leadership of
trained volunteers. Its purpose is exclusively educational and charitable.

INTRODUCTION

Come in and have a seat at the table, where a taste-tempting Michigan feast awaits you. No matter what the season, Michigan's bounty is sure to please. Whether it's fresh fish drawn from one of our great lakes, or juicy apples and cherries from our orchards, Michigan provides delicious delicacies year-round. The birthplace of the automobile, Michigan is home to many ethnic groups, from Polish and Italian to Middle Eastern and Greek. These groups in turn have provided a cultural smorgasbord of taste-tempting delights from around the world that slowly have been woven into the tapestry of Michigan cuisine. In *Seasons in Thyme,* we have captured this multiethnic array of culinary delights, as well as the delicacies that have been on our shores for many years.

Michigan has so much to offer the culinary world, no matter what the season. In the frigid winter, a warm beef pasty from the snow-blanketed Upper Peninsula is a hearty handheld meal sure to keep the chill away. A visit to the acclaimed cherry festival in Traverse City in the springtime yields a delicious crop of the juicy fruit for succulent cobblers and pies and for jams. Fresh whitefish caught from the shores of Lake Michigan on a warm summer's day result in a fabulous homegrown fish feast. And in autumn, orchards all over Michigan are bursting with sweet, crunchy apples that will soon turn into tart apple cider, pies, applesauce, and strudel. But perhaps the best way to enjoy Michigan apples is to visit a cider mill or orchard on a crisp fall day and take a crunchy bite out of hand.

You may want to work off some of the sumptuous menus that follow with a stroll through the Cranbrook Educational Community in Bloomfield Hills. This 315-acre National Landmark campus is one of the nation's greatest architectural complexes. With science exhibits, a planetarium, an art museum, and more than forty acres of gardens, Cranbrook offers a unique and memorable experience for visitors of all ages.

The Henry Ford Museum and Greenfield Village, in nearby Dearborn, are a wonderful educational experience for all, an actual monument to the living history of America. Greenfield Village boasts more than eighty historic buildings, including Thomas Edison's laboratory and the Wright Brothers' bicycle shop. Come and explore the village on foot and watch presenters in period costumes provide demonstrations about day-to-day life in early America.

When you visit the adjacent Henry Ford Museum, you will be amazed to see how life has changed over the past 300 years, with unique exhibits that showcase a slice of life in America. And what visit to the Motor City would be complete without visiting the history of the automobile exhibit?

Seasons in Thyme will take you to Michigan, to a scenic northern state of towering pine trees and ancient lighthouses, where every season provides a bounty of culinary delights. Within its pages, you will find delicious and stunning recipes perfect for any occasion—winter, spring, summer, and fall. Seasonal menus are also included, to help you plan authentic Michigan meals with a special touch.

All recipes have been triple-tested to ensure foolproof preparation and a delicious result we hope you will enjoy. For years, Michiganders have gathered around the table with family and friends to enjoy the homespun delights that are presented on these pages. It is our sincere hope that you do so as well.

Welcome to Michigan! We're so glad you've come.

JUNIOR LEAGUE OF
BIRMINGHAM, MICHIGAN

CONTENTS

SEASONAL MENUS

WINTER - *page 10*

A Snowflake by a recipe title indicates the recipe
is on a Winter menu.

SPRING - *page 14*

A Pansy by a recipe title indicates the recipe
is on a Spring menu.

SUMMER - *page 18*

A Sunflower by a recipe title indicates the recipe
is on a Summer menu.

FALL - *page 22*

An Oak Leaf by a recipe title indicates the recipe
is on a Fall menu.

CONTENTS

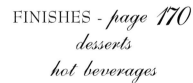

WINTER

In a way winter is the real spring,

the time when the inner things happen,

the resurge of nature.

—Edna O'Brien

DINNER FOR 4

Cranberry Relish - page 107

Maple-Glazed Cornish Game Hens - page 128

Wild Rice and Mushroom Stuffing - *page* 129

Caramelized Green Beans with Onion - page 96

Praline Pumpkin Pie with whipped cream - page 195

DINNER FOR 8

Green Salad with Onion Dressing - page 69

Lemon Sherry Chicken Supreme - page 120

Green Bean and Artichoke Casserole - page 95

Potatoes Poupon - page 99

Chocolate Pecan Pie - page 191

DINNER FOR 8

St. Patty's Favorite Corned Beef - page 142

Garlic Mashed Potatoes - page 101

Steamed Cabbage - page 142

Warm Apple Crisp - page 202

HORS D'OEUVRE PARTY

Chicken and Tart Cherry Won Tons - page 209

Lobster Rockefeller Hors d'Oeuvre - page 211

Roasted Pepper and Artichoke Tapenade - page 51

Smoked Salmon and Boursin Pinwheels - page 210

Toasted Almond Crab Spread - page 53

Stuffed Mushrooms - page 58

Miniature Beef Wellingtons - page 213

Wassail - page 203

SPRING

O Wind,

If Winter comes,

can Spring be far behind?

—Percy Bysshe Shelley

SIMPLE DINNER FOR 4

Lemon Thyme Chicken - page 118

Lemon Rice - page 104

Strawberry and Onion Salad - page 65

Caramel Bars - page 179

ELEGANT DINNER PARTY FOR 4

Asparagus Soup - page 81

Poached Salmon - page 131

Spring Risotto - page 105

Brown Derby Grapefruit Cake - page 227

DINNER FOR 6

Roasted Vegetable Caviar - page 52

Lamb Kabobs - page 147

Mediterranean Rice Salad - page 70

Orange Pie - page 193

BRUNCH FEAST

Spiral-cut ham

Breakfast Soufflé - page 42

Breakfast Orange Rolls - page 40

Raspberry Streusel Muffins - page 34

Lemon Nut Bread - page 30

Spinach and Chèvre Quiche - page 44

Asparagus Quiche - page 43

SUMMER

Rest is not idleness, and to lie

sometimes on the grass on a summer day

listening to the murmur of water, or

watching the clouds float across the sky,

is hardly a waste of time.

—John Lubbock

CASUAL DINNER FOR 6

Caprese Salad - page 70

Marinated Shrimp Barbecue - page 133

Artichoke Linguini - page 160

Frozen Strawberry Chantilly - page 198

ELEGANT SUMMER NIGHT
DINNER PARTY FOR 8

Tomato Basil Tartlets - page 56

Smoked Whitefish Spread with assorted crackers - page 54

Cold Cucumber Scandia - page 80

Michigan Cherry and Mixed Green Salad - page 64

Lamb Chops with Lemon and Thyme - page 146

Confetti Vegetables - page 97

Boiled new potatoes with browned butter

Peach Melba Pie - page 194

SUMMER SUPPER FOR 4

Goat Cheese Bruschetta - page 55

Warm Prosciutto and Parmesan Salad - page 67

Sun-Dried Tomato and Spinach Pasta - page 161

Cherry Orchard Pie - page 192

SUMMER LUNCHEON FOR 4

Chicken and Rice Asparagus Salad - page 74

Spinach Salad with Orange Dressing - page 71

Lemon Ice - page 198

Cream Wafers - page 182

FALL

Delicious autumn! My very soul is

wedded to it, and if I were a bird I

would fly about the earth seeking the

successive autumns.

—George Eliot

DINNER PARTY FOR 4

Caesar Salad - page 68

Herbed Ravioli with Pink Tomato Sauce - page 162

Scaloppine alla Marsala - page 143

Italian Spinach - page 101

Lemon Cake - page 177

FALL FEAST FOR 8

Golden Apple Salad - page 63

Michigan Cherry and Hard Cider Chicken - page 121

Wild rice

Stuffed Squash Florentine - page 102

Carrot Cake - page 172

ELEGANT DINNER PARTY FOR 6

Spinach-Stuffed Beef Tenderloin - page 139

Minnesota Rice - page 104

Dilled Carrots - page 97

Chocolate Hazelnut Torte - page 196

DINNER PARTY FOR 6

Butternut Squash and Creamy Cider Soup - page 83

Breaded Pork Tenderloin - page 148

Cranberry and Apple Chutney - page 149

Spinach Twice-Baked Potatoes - page 100

Gingerbread Cake with whipped cream - page 176

AWAKENINGS

breads

breakfast

JUNIOR LEAGUE OF
BIRMINGHAM, MICHIGAN

Best-Ever Banana Bread

2¹/₂ cups flour
1 teaspoon salt
1 teaspoon baking powder
2 teaspoons baking soda
1 cup (2 sticks) butter, softened
2 cups sugar
4 eggs
2 cups mashed bananas (about 6 bananas)
1 cup coarsely chopped walnuts

Mix the flour, salt, baking powder and baking soda together. Cream the butter
and sugar in a large bowl with an electric mixer until light and fluffy. Beat in the
eggs 1 at a time. Stir in the bananas and walnuts. Add the flour mixture gradually,
mixing well after each addition.

Spoon half the batter into each of 2 greased and floured 4x8-inch loaf pans. Bake
at 350 degrees for 50 to 60 minutes, or until a wooden pick inserted near the
center of the loaves comes out clean. Cool in the pans for 5 minutes. Remove to a
wire rack to cool completely.

Makes 2 loaves

Pictured on overleaf: Swedish Pancake (page 36)

Cranberry Bread

2 cups flour
2 teaspoons baking powder
1/4 teaspoon salt
1/2 cup shortening
1/2 teaspoon vanilla extract
1 cup sugar
1 egg
3/4 cup milk
1 cup fresh cranberries, rinsed and halved
1 cup chopped walnuts
Sugar to taste

Sift the flour, baking powder and salt together. Cream the shortening and vanilla in a bowl with an electric mixer. Add 1 cup sugar and beat until smooth. Beat in the egg. Add the flour mixture and milk alternately to the creamed mixture, mixing well after each addition. Fold in the cranberries and walnuts. Spoon the batter into a greased 5x9-inch loaf pan. Sprinkle with sugar. Bake at 350 degrees for 50 to 55 minutes. Serve warm.

Note: For a different flavor, try adding 2 tablespoons grated orange zest to the batter.

Makes 1 loaf

Lemon Nut Bread

1 1/4 cups flour
1 teaspoon baking powder
1/4 teaspoon salt
1/2 cup (1 stick) butter, softened, or 1/2 cup vegetable shortening
1 cup sugar
2 eggs, lightly beaten
1/2 cup milk
1/2 cup chopped walnuts
Grated zest of 1 lemon
1/4 cup sugar
Juice of 1 lemon

Mix the flour, baking powder and salt together. Cream the butter and 1 cup sugar in a bowl with an electric mixer until light and fluffy. Beat in the eggs. Add the flour mixture and milk alternately to the creamed mixture, mixing well after each addition. Fold in the walnuts and lemon zest.

Spoon the batter into a buttered loaf pan. Bake at 350 degrees for 1 hour. Remove from the oven and pierce the loaf in several places with a wooden pick.

Mix 1/4 cup sugar and the lemon juice in a small bowl. Pierce loaf in several places with a wooden pick. Pour the glaze over the hot bread. Let stand until cool. Remove from the pan and slice thinly to serve.

Makes 1 loaf

Harvest Pumpkin Pineapple Loaf

3¹/₂ cups flour
2 teaspoons baking soda
2 teaspoons pumpkin pie spice
1 teaspoon salt
2¹/₂ cups sugar
¹/₂ cup (1 stick) butter, softened
1 (15-ounce) can pumpkin
1 (8-ounce) can crushed pineapple
4 eggs
Confectioners' sugar to taste

Mix the flour, baking soda, pumpkin pie spice and salt together. Cream the sugar and butter in a bowl with an electric mixer until light and fluffy. Add the pumpkin, undrained pineapple and eggs and mix well. Add the flour mixture gradually, mixing well after each addition.

Spoon half the batter into each of two nonstick 4x8-inch loaf pans. Bake at 350 degrees for 55 to 65 minutes, or until the loaves test done. Cool in the pans for 5 minutes. Remove to a wire rack to cool completely. Sprinkle the loaves with confectioners' sugar.

Makes 2 loaves

Apple Bran Muffins

1/4 cup wheat germ
1 1/2 cups 100% bran cereal
1 1/3 cups milk
1 1/4 cups flour
1/2 cup sugar
1/2 teaspoon salt
1 teaspoon cinnamon
1 tablespoon baking powder
1 egg
1/3 cup vegetable oil or honey
2 cups chopped apples
1/2 cup raisins
1/2 cup chopped walnuts

Soak the wheat germ and cereal in the milk in a bowl for 10 minutes. Mix the flour, sugar, salt, cinnamon and baking powder together. Add the egg and vegetable oil to the cereal mixture and mix well. Add the flour mixture gradually, mixing after each addition. Fold in the apples, raisins and walnuts.

Fill greased muffin cups 1/2 full with batter. Bake at 400 degrees for 25 to 30 minutes, or until the muffins test done.

Makes 1 dozen

Pumpkin Muffins

1/2 teaspoon salt
1/2 teaspoon baking powder
1 1/2 teaspoons ground cloves
2 teaspoons baking soda
1 tablespoon cinnamon
3 1/3 cups flour
2 2/3 cups sugar
2/3 cup vegetable oil
4 eggs, beaten
2 cups mashed cooked pumpkin, or 1 large can pumpkin
2/3 cup water

Mix the salt, baking powder, cloves, baking soda, cinnamon and flour in a bowl. Cream the sugar and vegetable oil in a bowl with an electric mixer until light and fluffy. Add the eggs, pumpkin and water and mix well. Add the flour mixture gradually, mixing after each addition. Spoon the batter into nonstick muffin cups. Bake at 350 degrees for 30 minutes.

Makes 3 dozen

Raspberry Streusel Muffins

Streusel Topping

1/2 cup flour
1/2 cup quick-cooking oats
1/3 cup sugar

1/2 teaspoon cinnamon
1/8 teaspoon salt
6 tablespoons butter

Batter

2 cups flour
1/2 teaspoon baking powder
1/2 teaspoon baking soda
1/2 teaspoon cinnamon
1/4 teaspoon salt
1/2 cup (1 stick) butter, softened
1/2 cup sugar

1 egg
1/2 cup milk
1/2 cup sour cream
1 teaspoon vanilla extract
1 cup fresh raspberries, or 1 cup
    drained thawed frozen raspberries

Assembly

Confectioners' sugar to taste

For the streusel topping, mix the flour, oats, sugar, cinnamon and salt in a medium bowl. Cut in the butter until crumbly. Rub the mixture between the fingers to break up large pieces. Set aside.

For the batter, mix the flour, baking powder, baking soda, cinnamon and salt together. Cream the butter and sugar in a bowl with an electric mixer until light and fluffy. Beat in the egg. Mix the milk, sour cream and vanilla in a bowl. Add the flour mixture and milk mixture alternately to the creamed mixture, mixing after each addition. Fold in the raspberries.

To assemble, fill greased muffin cups 2/3 full with batter. Sprinkle each muffin generously with streusel topping. Bake at 400 degrees for 20 to 25 minutes, or until a wooden pick inserted near the center comes out clean. Cool in the pan on a wire rack for 5 minutes. Remove from the pan. Sprinkle with confectioners' sugar.

Makes 1 dozen

Pear-Stuffed French Toast

6 eggs
1¹/2 cups milk
¹/2 cup orange juice
¹/4 cup Poire William (pear-flavored liqueur)
2 tablespoons lemon juice
2 tablespoons sugar

¹/8 teaspoon salt
Zest of 1 orange
Zest of 1 lemon
6 thick slices bread
Sautéed Pears (below)
Vegetable oil for frying
Warm maple syrup (optional)

Combine the eggs, milk, orange juice, liqueur, lemon juice, sugar, salt, orange zest and lemon zest in a wide deep dish. Mix with a fork.

Dip the bread slices into the egg mixture until moistened but not sopping. Place the bread on a plate. Cover 3 of the bread slices with the sautéed pears. Top each with another bread slice to form sandwiches.

Pour about ¹/8-inch vegetable oil into a large skillet, tilting to coat the skillet. Heat over medium-high heat until a drop of water sizzles in the oil. Using a spatula, carefully slide the sandwiches from the plate into the skillet. Cook until golden brown on 1 side. Turn and cook until golden brown and slightly puffy throughout. Drain on paper towels. Serve hot with warm maple syrup.

Makes 3 servings

Sautéed Pears

1 tablespoon butter
3 medium Bosc pears, cored and thinly sliced
1 tablespoon sugar

Melt the butter in a large skillet over medium-high heat. Add the pears and sugar. Cook for 10 minutes, or until the pears are tender and caramelized.

Makes 3 servings

Swedish Pancake

*Topped with fresh fruit, this pancake makes a very pretty presentation.
It makes a filling breakfast for two or part of breakfast for four.*

3 tablespoons butter
2 eggs
1/2 cup milk
1/2 cup flour
1/4 teaspoon nutmeg
Sliced fresh fruit, such as peaches, berries or bananas
Brown sugar to taste
Cream

Melt the butter in a baking dish, being careful not to let it brown. Beat the eggs in a bowl with a whisk. Add the milk, flour and nutmeg and mix until smooth.

Pour the batter into the baking dish. Bake at 425 degrees for 10 to 15 minutes, or until the pancake is puffed and light golden brown.

Remove the pancake to a serving dish. Cover with fruit and sprinkle with brown sugar. Pour a small amount of cream over the top. Serve hot.

Makes 2 to 4 servings

Almond Apricot Coffee Cake

2 cups flour
1 teaspoon baking powder
1/4 teaspoon salt
1 cup (2 sticks) butter, softened
2 cups sugar
3 eggs
1 cup sour cream
1 teaspoon almond extract
3/4 cup slivered almonds
6 ounces apricot preserves

Mix the flour, baking powder and salt together. Cream the butter and sugar in a bowl with an electric mixer until light and fluffy. Add the eggs, sour cream and almond extract and mix well. Add the flour mixture gradually, mixing after each addition.

Spread half the batter in a greased and floured bundt pan. Sprinkle with half the almonds. Spread the preserves over the top, leaving a 1/2-inch margin around the edge. Spread with the remaining batter. Top with the remaining almonds. Bake at 350 degrees for 1 hour. Cool in the pan for 15 minutes. Invert onto a serving plate.

Makes 16 servings

Polish Doughnuts (Paczki)

2 envelopes yeast
1 teaspoon salt
1 1/2 cups milk, scalded and cooled
1/2 cup sugar
1/2 cup (1 stick) butter, softened
1 egg
3 egg yolks
1 teaspoon vanilla extract
1/2 teaspoon nutmeg (optional)
4 1/2 cups flour
Vegetable oil for deep-frying
Sugar or cinnamon sugar to taste

Sprinkle the yeast and salt over the cooled milk. Cream 1/2 cup sugar and the butter in a bowl with an electric mixer until light and fluffy. Add the egg, egg yolks, vanilla and nutmeg and beat until smooth. Add the flour gradually and beat until a smooth dough forms. Add the milk mixture and mix well.

Cover the dough and let rise in a warm place until doubled in bulk. Shape the dough into small balls. Arrange on waxed paper and let rise again.

Deep-fry the dough in hot vegetable oil until golden brown. Remove with a slotted spoon and drain on paper towels. Sprinkle cooled doughnuts with sugar.

Makes 3 dozen

Dried Cherry Scones

2 cups flour
1/3 cup sugar
2 teaspoons baking powder
1/4 teaspoon salt
1/3 cup chilled butter, cut into pieces
1 egg
2/3 cup cream
1 teaspoon vanilla extract
1 teaspoon almond extract
1 cup dried cherries
1 egg, beaten
1 teaspoon water
Sugar to taste
Sliced almonds

Mix the flour, 1/3 cup sugar, the baking powder and salt in a bowl. Cut in the butter with a pastry blender. Mix 1 egg, the cream, vanilla extract and almond extract in a bowl. Add the flour mixture gradually, mixing after each addition. Add the cherries and mix well; the dough will be very sticky.

Using floured hands, knead the dough 4 or 5 times on a floured surface. Pat 1/2-inch thick. Cut out circles with a biscuit cutter or cookie cutter. Brush the tops with a mixture of 1 egg and the water. Sprinkle with sugar and almonds. Place on a greased baking sheet. Bake at 325 degrees for 15 to 18 minutes, or until golden brown.

Makes 8 servings

Breakfast Orange Rolls

Dough

1 cake yeast
1/4 cup lukewarm water
1/4 cup sugar
1 teaspoon salt
2 eggs
1/2 cup sour cream

1/2 cup (1 stick) butter, melted
2 1/2 to 3 cups flour
3/4 cup sugar
3/4 cup flaked coconut
2 1/2 tablespoons grated orange zest
1/4 cup (1/2 stick) butter, melted

Orange Glaze

3/4 cup sugar
1/2 cup sour cream
2 tablespoons orange juice

1/4 cup (1/2 stick) butter
1/2 cup coconut, toasted

For the dough, soften the yeast in the lukewarm water in a large mixing bowl. Stir in 1/4 cup sugar, the salt, eggs, sour cream and 1/2 cup butter. Add enough of the flour gradually to make a stiff dough, beating after each addition. Let rise, covered, until doubled in bulk.

Mix 3/4 cup sugar, the coconut and orange zest in a small bowl. Knead the dough on a floured surface. Divide into 3 equal portions. Roll 1 portion into a 10-inch circle. Brush generously with some of the 1/4 cup melted butter. Sprinkle with 1/3 of the coconut mixture. Cut into 12 wedges and roll up from the wide end. Repeat with the remaining portions of dough.

Place the rolls point side down in 3 rows in a greased 9x13-inch baking pan. Cover and let rise in a warm place until almost doubled in bulk. Bake at 350 degrees for 25 to 30 minutes, or until golden brown.

For the glaze, combine the sugar, sour cream, orange juice and butter in a small saucepan. Boil for 3 minutes. Pour over the hot rolls in the pan. Sprinkle with the coconut.

Makes 3 dozen

Pecan Coconut Breakfast Rolls

1/3 cup butter
1/2 cup packed brown sugar
3 tablespoons sour cream
1 cup puffed rice cereal
1/2 cup chopped pecans
1/2 cup flaked coconut
3 ounces cream cheese, softened
1/4 cup confectioners' sugar
1/4 teaspoon vanilla extract
1 (17-ounce) package puff pastry, cut into 8 pieces, or
    1 (8-count) can refrigerator crescent rolls

Melt the butter and brown sugar in a saucepan. Cook for 2 minutes, stirring constantly. Add the sour cream and cook for 1 minute. Stir in the cereal, pecans and coconut. Blend the cream cheese, confectioners' sugar and vanilla in a bowl.

Press each pastry piece over the bottom and up the side of a nonstick muffin cup. Spoon equal amounts of the cream cheese mixture into each muffin cup. Top each with the pecan mixture.

Bake at 350 degrees for 11 to 16 minutes, or until golden brown. Cool in the muffin cups for 5 minutes. Serve hot.

Makes 8 servings

Breakfast Soufflé

12 slices bread, crusts removed
1/2 cup (1 stick) butter, melted
1/8 teaspoon garlic powder
8 ounces sharp Cheddar cheese, shredded
8 ounces mild Cheddar cheese, shredded
6 eggs, beaten
3 cups milk
12 ounces bacon, crisp-cooked and crumbled

Cut the bread into crouton-size cubes. Combine the butter and garlic powder in a large bowl and mix well. Add the bread cubes and toss until coated. Place the bread cubes in a greased 9x13-inch casserole. Top with all the cheese. Combine the eggs and milk in a bowl and beat until blended. Pour over the cheese. Chill, covered, in the refrigerator overnight. Bake at 325 degrees for 30 minutes. Sprinkle with the bacon. Bake for 15 minutes longer.

Makes 10 to 12 servings

Quiche Bites

2 cups (8 ounces) shredded Monterey Jack cheese or sharp Cheddar cheese
2 cups (8 ounces) shredded Swiss cheese
8 slices bacon, crisp-cooked and crumbled
1/4 cup sliced green onions
3 eggs, beaten
1/4 cup milk

Combine the cheeses, bacon and green onions in a bowl. Add the eggs and milk and mix well. Spoon into an 8-inch-square baking dish. Bake at 350 degrees for 25 to 30 minutes. Cut into squares. Serve with crackers. If desired, add chopped red or yellow bell peppers.

Makes 16 servings

Soufflé Lorraine

4 eggs, separated
16 ounces cottage cheese
1/2 cup (2 ounces) grated Parmesan
   cheese
1/3 cup cream

3 tablespoons flour
6 slices bacon, crisp-cooked and
   crumbled
1/8 teaspoon pepper, or to taste

Beat the egg whites in a bowl with an electric mixer until stiff but not dry; set aside. Beat the egg yolks in a bowl with a mixer until thick and pale yellow. Beat in the cottage cheese, Parmesan cheese, cream and flour. Stir in the bacon and pepper. Fold in the egg whites. Spoon into a buttered 1 1/2-quart soufflé dish. Bake at 300 degrees for 60 to 65 minutes, or until a knife inserted near the center comes out clean. Let stand for 5 minutes before serving.

Makes 4 servings

Asparagus Quiche

1 unbaked pie pastry, prepared from
   Basic Pie Crust recipe (page 192)
1 1/2 cups (6 ounces) shredded smoked
   Gouda cheese
1 pound asparagus pieces, cooked

1 cup chopped smoked turkey or ham
6 eggs
3/4 cup milk
Salt and pepper to taste

Fit the pie pastry into a pie plate. Sprinkle the cheese over the bottom of the pastry. Arrange the asparagus over the cheese. Top with the turkey. Beat the eggs lightly in a bowl. Add the milk and mix well. Season with salt and pepper. Pour over the asparagus. Bake at 375 degrees for 45 minutes. Let stand for 10 minutes before slicing.

Makes 6 servings

Spinach and Chèvre Quiche

Pastry

1/2 cup (1 stick) unsalted butter
1 1/4 cups flour

1 egg yolk
1 1/2 to 2 tablespoons ice water

Filling

2 tablespoons butter
2 green onions, chopped
2 (10-ounce) packages frozen chopped
 spinach, thawed and drained, or
 24 ounces fresh spinach
3 eggs
1/2 cup cream or half-and-half
1/4 teaspoon nutmeg

1/2 teaspoon salt
1/4 teaspoon freshly ground pepper
2 tablespoons minced fresh parsley
3/4 cup (3 ounces) crumbled chèvre
 cheese or feta cheese
1/2 cup (2 ounces) freshly grated
 Parmesan cheese

Assembly

1 tablespoon Dijon mustard

For the pastry, cut the butter into the flour in a mixing bowl. Add the egg yolk and mix lightly with a fork. Add the ice water gradually, mixing until the dough forms a ball. Roll into a 13-inch circle on a lightly floured board. Fit into a quiche dish. Chill in the refrigerator for 15 minutes or longer.

For the filling, melt the butter in a skillet over medium heat. Add the green onions and sauté for 1 to 2 minutes. Add the spinach. Cook until frozen spinach is heated through or fresh spinach is tender. Remove from the heat and squeeze any excess moisture from the mixture.

Beat the eggs in a mixing bowl. Add the cream, nutmeg, salt, pepper, parsley, spinach mixture and chèvre cheese and mix well.

To assemble, spread the pastry with the Dijon mustard. Spoon the egg mixture into the prepared crust. Bake at 400 degrees for 10 minutes. Reduce the oven temperature to 350 degrees. Bake for 25 to 35 minutes, or until a knife inserted near the center comes out clean. Sprinkle with the Parmesan cheese during the last 15 minutes of baking time. Serve warm.

Makes 8 servings

Breakfast Sausage Roll

1 pound bulk sausage
1 cup (4 ounces) shredded Cheddar cheese
2 eggs
1 teaspoon chopped fresh parsley
2 cans refrigerator crescent rolls
1 egg, beaten

Brown the sausage in a skillet, stirring until crumbly; drain well. Add the cheese, 2 eggs and the parsley and mix well. Unroll the crescent roll dough onto a baking sheet, placing them with 1 long side together. Press together, sealing the perforations. Spoon the sausage mixture down the roll, slightly off center. Pull 1 side of the dough over the top, pinching all 3 remaining edges together and sealing the sausage mixture inside. Cut several slits to vent. Brush with the beaten egg. Bake at 350 degrees for 30 minutes. Slice as for a loaf of bread and serve warm.

Makes 10 servings

Banana Berry Smoothies

3/4 cup buttermilk or low-fat milk
1/2 cup nonfat vanilla yogurt
1/2 banana, cut into chunks
3 strawberries
2 teaspoons honey
2 ice cubes

Combine the buttermilk, yogurt, banana, strawberries and honey in a blender. Process at high speed until blended and smooth. With the blender running, add the ice cubes 1 at a time. Process until smooth and frothy. Pour into chilled large glasses. Serve immediately.

Makes 2 servings

STARTERS

appetizers

salads

soups

cold drinks

Bleu Cheese Spread with Walnuts

1 pound cream cheese, softened
5 ounces bleu cheese
1 cup walnut halves, chopped
1/4 cup chopped green onions
Salt and pepper to taste
Toasted sliced bread or crackers

Combine the cream cheese, bleu cheese, walnuts, green onions, salt and pepper in a bowl and mix well. Serve with toasted sliced bread or crackers.

Makes 8 servings

Kahlúa Pecan Brie

3/4 tablespoon packed brown sugar
1/4 cup Kahlúa
3/4 cup pecan halves, toasted
1 (17-ounce) package puff pastry
1 (16-ounce) wheel brie cheese
Fresh fruit (optional)

Combine the brown sugar and Kahlúa in a small skillet. Heat until the brown sugar is dissolved, stirring constantly until blended. Add the pecans and simmer until the mixture is heated through but not runny. Remove from the heat. Place the puff pastry on a baking sheet. Place the brie wheel on the puff pastry sheet. Spoon the pecan mixture over the top of the cheese. Wrap the pastry around the cheese, pinching together to seal any holes. Bake at 375 degrees for 15 to 20 minutes, or until golden brown. Garnish with fresh fruit, such as grapes or pears.

Note: You can unwrap one sheet of the puff pastry and return the other sheet to the freezer. Thaw the pastry at room temperature for 30 minutes on a baking sheet. Unfold the pastry on the baking sheet.

Makes 8 to 10 servings

*Pictured on overleaf: Warm Prosciutto and Parmesan Salad (page 67) and
Butternut Squash and Creamy Cider Soup (page 83)*

Hot Olive Cheese Balls

1 cup (4 ounces) shredded sharp Cheddar cheese
3 tablespoons butter, softened
1/2 teaspoon Worcestershire sauce
1/2 cup sifted flour
1/4 teaspoon salt
1/2 teaspoon cayenne pepper
1 jar pimento-stuffed green olives

Mix the cheese and butter in a bowl. Stir in the Worcestershire sauce, flour, salt
and cayenne pepper. Press a small amount of the cheese mixture around each olive,
completely covering each olive. Place the olives on an ungreased baking sheet; the
olives should not be touching. Bake at 400 degrees for 10 to 15 minutes, or until
golden brown. Serve warm. Unbaked cheese balls can be frozen.

Makes 6 servings

Garlic Feta Cheese Spread

4 ounces feta cheese, crumbled
4 ounces reduced-fat cream cheese, softened
1/3 cup light mayonnaise
1 garlic clove, minced
1/4 teaspoon basil, crushed
1/4 teaspoon oregano, crushed
1/8 teaspoon dillweed
1/8 teaspoon thyme, crushed
Sprigs of fresh thyme (optional)
Assorted fresh vegetables
Unsalted crackers or pita rounds

Combine the feta cheese, cream cheese, mayonnaise, garlic, basil, oregano, dillweed
and thyme in a mixing bowl or food processor. Beat at medium speed until mixed.
Chill, covered, until serving time. Garnish the spread with fresh thyme. Serve with
assorted vegetables and unsalted crackers or pita rounds.

Makes 1 1/2 cups

Pesto and Sun-Dried Tomato Torte

6 to 8 ounces sun-dried tomatoes
2 cups fresh basil
1/2 cup fresh parsley
1/2 cup (2 ounces) grated Romano
  cheese
2 garlic cloves

1/4 cup olive oil
1/4 cup pine nuts
12 ounces cream cheese, softened
1/2 cup (1 stick) butter, softened
Water crackers

Soak the sun-dried tomatoes in boiling water in a bowl for 2 to 5 minutes; drain well. Chop the tomatoes and set aside. Combine the basil, parsley, Romano cheese, garlic, olive oil and pine nuts in a blender and process until chopped. Pour into a bowl and set aside. Combine the cream cheese and butter in a blender and process until blended and smooth. Line a small bowl with plastic wrap, leaving an overhang. Layer the cream cheese mixture, basil mixture and tomatoes 1/2 at a time in the bowl. Fold the plastic over the top. Chill for 2 hours or longer. Invert onto a plate. Serve with water crackers.

Makes 8 to 10 servings

Hot Vegetable Dip

7 slices bacon, chopped
2 garlic cloves, minced
8 ounces cream cheese, softened
1/4 cup half-and-half
4 ounces bleu cheese, crumbled

2 tablespoons chopped chives
  (optional)
3 tablespoons slivered almonds
Fresh vegetables or crackers

Cook the bacon in a skillet until crisp. Stir in the garlic; drain well. Beat the cream cheese in a bowl with an electric mixer until smooth. Blend in the half-and-half. Stir in the bacon mixture, bleu cheese and chives. Spoon into a baking dish. Sprinkle with the almonds. Bake, covered with foil, at 350 degrees for 20 to 30 minutes, or until heated through. Serve hot with fresh vegetables or crackers.

Makes 6 to 8 servings

Jalapeño Artichoke Spread

1 (14-ounce) can artichoke hearts, chopped
1/2 cup mayonnaise
1 cup (4 ounces) grated Parmesan cheese
8 ounces cream cheese, softened
1/4 teaspoon garlic powder
2 to 3 jalapeño chiles, chopped
1 Boboli pizza crust

Mix the artichoke hearts, mayonnaise, Parmesan cheese, cream cheese, garlic powder and jalapeños in a bowl. Spread over the pizza crust. Bake at 350 degrees for 10 minutes. Cut into wedges and serve hot.

Makes 6 to 8 servings

Roasted Pepper and Artichoke Tapenade

1 (7-ounce) jar roasted red bell peppers, drained and coarsely chopped
1 (6-ounce) jar marinated artichoke hearts, drained and coarsely chopped
1/2 cup minced fresh parsley
1/2 cup (2 ounces) freshly grated Parmesan cheese
1/3 cup olive oil
1/4 cup drained capers
4 garlic cloves, chopped
1 tablespoon fresh lemon juice
Salt and pepper to taste
Crackers or toasted pita triangles

Combine the bell peppers, artichoke hearts, parsley, cheese, olive oil, capers, garlic and lemon juice in a food processor. Pulse until the mixture is finely chopped. Pour into a bowl. Season with salt and pepper. May be prepared 1 day ahead and kept, covered, in the refrigerator. Serve with crackers or toasted pita triangles.

Makes about 1 3/4 cups

Favorite Spinach Spread

1 (10-ounce) package frozen chopped spinach
1/2 cup minced fresh parsley
1 tablespoon minced onion
1/3 cup mayonnaise
2 tablespoons sour cream
Salt and pepper to taste
Nacho chips

Parsley is the most widely used culinary herb in the United States. It is high in vitamins A and C and contains iron, iodine, and copper.

Cook the spinach in boiling water in a saucepan just until tender; drain well. Combine the spinach, parsley, onion, mayonnaise and sour cream in a bowl and mix well. Season with salt and pepper. Chill, covered, for 1 hour or longer to allow flavors to blend. Serve with nacho chips.

Makes 8 to 10 servings

Roasted Vegetable Caviar

1 medium plum tomato, halved and seeded
1 small yellow bell pepper, coarsely chopped
1 small onion, coarsely chopped
1 small yellow summer squash or zucchini, chopped
1 large carrot, chopped
1/8 teaspoon garlic powder, or to taste
1 tablespoon olive oil
2 teaspoons red wine vinegar
1/4 teaspoon salt
1/4 teaspoon Tabasco sauce
Tortilla chips or pita chips

Place the tomato, bell pepper, onion, squash and carrot in a 9x13-inch baking pan. Sprinkle with the garlic powder. Drizzle the olive oil over the vegetables, stirring to coat the vegetables. Bake at 425 degrees for 30 minutes, stirring once. Remove from the oven and let cool. Remove to a food processor. Pulse until coarsely chopped. Stir in the vinegar, salt and Tabasco sauce. Serve with tortilla chips or pita chips.

Makes about 2 cups

Zesty Sun-Dried Tomato Pesto

1 cup boiling water
1 cup sun-dried tomatoes (about 2 ounces)
1/2 cup firmly packed fresh basil
1/3 cup firmly packed fresh parsley
3 garlic cloves, halved
1/4 teaspoon salt
1/8 teaspoon cayenne pepper, or to taste
Crostini or grilled vegetables

Pour the boiling water over the tomatoes in a bowl. Let stand, covered with plastic wrap, for 1 hour. Process the basil and parsley in a blender until mixed well. Add the undrained tomatoes and garlic and purée until smooth. Pour into a small bowl. Season with the salt and cayenne pepper. Cover and chill thoroughly. Serve at room temperature on crostini or grilled vegetables. Do not use oil-packed sun-dried tomatoes in this recipe.

Makes 1 1/4 cups

Toasted Almond Crab Spread

8 ounces cream cheese, softened
1 1/2 cups (6 ounces) shredded Swiss cheese
1/3 cup sour cream
1/8 teaspoon nutmeg
1/8 teaspoon pepper
1 (6-ounce) can crab meat, drained and flaked
2 tablespoons chopped green onions
1/3 cup sliced almonds, toasted
1 tablespoon chopped green onions
Assorted crackers

Combine the cream cheese, Swiss cheese, sour cream, nutmeg and pepper in a bowl and mix well. Stir in the crab meat and 2 tablespoons green onions. Spread in a 9-inch pie plate. Bake at 350 degrees for 15 minutes or until heated through. Sprinkle with the almonds and 1 tablespoon green onions. Serve with crackers.

Makes 2 cups

Smoked Whitefish Spread

8 ounces cream cheese, softened
1 cup smoked whitefish, flaked
1/8 teaspoon pepper
1/2 teaspoon dillweed
1/4 teaspoon lemon juice
1 teaspoon brown sugar
Crackers

Combine the cream cheese, whitefish, pepper, dillweed, lemon juice and brown sugar in a food processor. Process until mixed well. Serve with crackers.

Makes about 2 cups

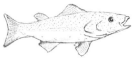

"No human being ever wearied of good fresh northern whitefish; no human being was ever made ill by eating too much of it."

—U.P. Hendrick,
The Land of the
Crooked Tree, *1948*

Crab Phyllo Bites

8 ounces cream cheese, softened
1/3 cup mayonnaise
3/4 cup (3 ounces) shredded Cheddar cheese
1/8 teaspoon cayenne pepper
1 large red bell pepper, finely chopped
1 (6-ounce) can crab meat, drained and flaked
45 miniature phyllo cups

Combine the cream cheese, mayonnaise, Cheddar cheese and cayenne pepper in a bowl and mix well. Fold in the bell pepper and crab meat. Place the phyllo cups on a baking sheet. Drop a rounded spoonful of the crab meat mixture into each cup. Bake at 300 degrees for 12 to 14 minutes, or until golden brown.

Makes 8 to 10 servings

Smoked Salmon Toasts

4 ounces smoked salmon, minced
1/2 cup (2 ounces) shredded mozzarella cheese
1/2 cup mayonnaise
1/4 cup finely chopped red onion
2 tablespoons drained rinsed capers
32 melba toast rounds
Chopped fresh parsley (optional)

Combine the salmon, cheese, mayonnaise, onion and capers in a bowl and mix well. Spread 1 teaspoonful of the mixture on each toast round. Place on a baking sheet. Bake at 350 degrees for 8 to 10 minutes or until heated through. Sprinkle with parsley and serve warm.

Makes 32 servings

Goat Cheese Bruschetta

8 to 10 plum tomatoes, chopped
1 bunch fresh basil, chopped
6 garlic cloves, minced
1/3 cup olive oil
2 tablespoons balsamic vinegar
Salt and pepper to taste
2 baguettes French bread, cut into 1 1/2-inch slices
1 (10-ounce) package goat cheese

Mix the tomatoes, basil, garlic, olive oil and vinegar in a bowl. Season with salt and pepper. Place the bread on a baking sheet and broil until golden brown on both sides. Let cool. Spread the goat cheese on each slice. Top each slice with a dollop of the tomato mixture. For added flavor, try stirring some pesto into the goat cheese.

Makes 16 to 20 servings

Peppers on Pumpernickel Toasts

2 yellow bell peppers, chopped
2 red bell peppers, chopped
1 to 1 1/2 cups mayonnaise or light mayonnaise
1 1/2 cups (6 ounces) grated Parmesan cheese
1/2 cup chopped onion
1 package cocktail pumpernickel bread

Combine the bell peppers, mayonnaise, cheese and onion in a bowl and mix well.
Spread on the bread slices. Place the slices on a baking sheet. Bake at 350 degrees
for 20 to 25 minutes or until the cheese is melted. Serve immediately.

Makes 15 to 20 servings

Tomato Basil Tartlets

4 ounces Swiss cheese, shredded
4 medium tomatoes, seeded and chopped
1/2 cup chopped basil
2 ounces black olives, chopped
Salt and pepper to taste
2 packages miniature phyllo cups

Mix the cheese, tomatoes, basil and olives in a bowl. Season with salt and pepper.
Spoon 2 teaspoons of the mixture into each phyllo cup. Place on a baking sheet.
Bake at 400 degrees for 25 to 30 minutes, or until the filling is set and the phyllo
cups are golden brown. Serve warm.

Makes 10 servings

Basil Tomato Cheese Tart

1 unbaked pie pastry, prepared from Basic Pie Crust recipe (page 192)
1/2 cup (2 ounces) shredded mozzarella cheese
1 cup chopped fresh basil
4 garlic cloves
5 Roma tomatoes, cut into wedges and drained
1 cup (4 ounces) shredded mozzarella cheese
1/2 to 3/4 cup mayonnaise or light mayonnaise
1/4 cup grated Parmesan cheese
1/4 cup grated asiago cheese
1/8 teaspoon white pepper

Fit the pie pastry into a 9-inch quiche dish or pie plate and flute the edge. Bake at 450 degrees for 5 to 7 minutes or until light golden brown. Remove from the oven and sprinkle 1/2 cup mozzarella cheese over the crust. Let cool.

Combine the basil and garlic in a food processor and process until coarsely chopped. Reserve 2 tablespoons of the mixture. Arrange the tomato wedges over the melted cheese in the pie crust. Sprinkle with the remaining basil mixture.

Combine 1 cup mozzarella cheese, the mayonnaise, Parmesan cheese, asiago cheese and pepper in a medium bowl and mix well. Spoon over the basil mixture in the pie crust, spreading evenly. Sprinkle with the reserved basil mixture.

Bake at 375 degrees for 35 to 40 minutes, or until the top is golden brown and bubbly. Cover the edge of the pie crust with foil if needed to prevent overbrowning. Cut into slices and serve hot.

Makes 6 to 8 servings

Stuffed Mushrooms

16 to 20 (or more) large mushrooms
6 slices bacon
1/4 cup minced onion
1/4 cup fine bread crumbs
1/2 teaspoon salt
1/8 teaspoon pepper
1 cup sour cream
1/4 teaspoon Worcestershire sauce

Mesick, in the northern lower portion of Michigan, is the mushroom capital of Michigan.

Clean the mushrooms and remove the stems. Chop the stems and set aside. Place the mushroom caps in a greased shallow baking pan. Brown the bacon in a skillet. Crumble the bacon and set aside. Sauté the onion and mushroom stems in the bacon drippings in the skillet until tender; drain well. Mix the onion mixture, bread crumbs, bacon, salt, pepper, sour cream and Worcestershire sauce in a bowl. Spoon into the mushroom caps. Bake at 350 degrees for 20 minutes.

Makes 16 to 20 servings

Killer Cocktail Cookies

7 tablespoons butter
1 cup flour
3 ounces Gorgonzola cheese, crumbled
2 teaspoons caraway seeds
Cracked pepper to taste

Cut the butter into the flour in a bowl until crumbly. Add the cheese and caraway seeds. Add a generous grinding of pepper and mix lightly. Shape into small balls and place on a cookie sheet. Flatten slightly in a crisscross pattern with a fork. Bake at 425 degrees for 8 to 10 minutes or until golden brown. Let cool before serving. May be frozen. These are delicious with wine and grapes.

Makes 24 to 30 servings

Asparagus Rolls with Three Cheeses

2 cups water
1/2 teaspoon salt
10 fresh asparagus spears, trimmed
4 ounces bleu cheese
1 ounce cream cheese, softened
1/4 cup (1/2 stick) unsalted butter,
   softened

1 teaspoon grated onion
10 slices thin white bread, crusts
   removed
1/4 cup (1/2 stick) unsalted butter,
   melted
1/2 cup grated Parmigiano-Reggiano
   cheese

Bring the water and salt to a boil in a large heavy saucepan. Add the asparagus. Cook, covered, for 3 to 5 minutes or just until tender-crisp; drain well. Combine the bleu cheese, cream cheese, softened butter and onion in a food processor and process until mixed well. Roll each bread slice 1/8-inch thick. Spread each with the cheese mixture. Place 1 asparagus spear in the center of each bread slice and roll up. Trim away any bits of asparagus that extend past the bread. Brush the rolls with the melted butter and coat with the Parmigiano-Reggiano cheese. Place on a baking sheet. Bake at 350 degrees for 15 to 20 minutes, or until lightly browned. Cut the rolls into thirds to serve.

Makes 30 rolls

Bacon-Wrapped Asparagus

1 pound sliced bacon
16 to 18 asparagus spears
16 to 18 slices thin white bread

6 ounces cream cheese, softened
1/8 teaspoon cayenne pepper, or
   to taste

Cut each bacon slice in half crosswise and set aside. Cook the asparagus in boiling water in a saucepan for 4 to 6 minutes or just until tender-crisp. Roll each bread slice 1/8-inch thick. Mix the cream cheese and cayenne pepper in a bowl. Spread a thin layer of the cream cheese mixture on each bread slice. Place 1 asparagus spear at the edge of each bread slice and roll up. Trim away any bits of asparagus that extend past the bread. Cut each roll into halves. Wrap 1 piece of bacon around each roll, securing with a wooden pick. Place on a wire rack set on a baking sheet. Bake at 400 degrees for 15 to 20 minutes, or until the bacon is cooked through. Serve immediately. Unbaked rolls can be frozen.

Makes 32 to 36 rolls

Spinach and Artichokes in Puff Pastry

1 (17-ounce) package frozen puff pastry
1 (10-ounce) package frozen chopped spinach, thawed and drained
1 (14-ounce) can artichoke hearts, drained and chopped
1/2 cup mayonnaise
1/2 cup grated Parmesan cheese
1 teaspoon onion powder
1 teaspoon garlic powder
1/2 teaspoon pepper

Thaw the puff pastry at room temperature for 30 minutes. Combine the spinach, artichoke hearts, mayonnaise, cheese, onion powder, garlic powder and pepper in a bowl and mix well. Unfold the puff pastry and place on heavy-duty plastic wrap.

Spread half the spinach mixture evenly over 1 pastry sheet, leaving a 1/2-inch border. Roll up the pastry as for a jelly roll, pressing to seal the seam. Wrap in plastic wrap. Repeat with the remaining pastry sheet and spinach mixture.

Freeze the pastry rolls for 30 minutes. Cut into 1/2-inch slices and place on a baking sheet. Bake at 400 degrees for 20 minutes, or until golden brown.

Note: The unbaked rolls can be frozen for up to 3 months, making them perfect for a make-ahead appetizer to keep on hand. Thaw for 1 hour before slicing and baking.

Makes 4 dozen

Chicken Satay

Marinade

3/4 cup fresh lemon juice
   (about 4 lemons)
3/4 cup olive oil
2 teaspoons kosher salt
1 teaspoon freshly ground pepper

1 tablespoon minced fresh thyme, or
   1/2 teaspoon dried thyme
2 pounds boneless skinless chicken
   breasts

Satay

1 tablespoon olive oil
1 tablespoon dark sesame oil or
   toasted sesame oil
2/3 cup chopped red onion
1 1/2 teaspoons minced garlic
1 1/2 teaspoons minced fresh gingerroot
1/4 teaspoon crushed red pepper flakes

2 tablespoons red wine vinegar
1/4 cup packed light brown sugar
2 tablespoons soy sauce
1/2 cup creamy peanut butter
1/4 cup ketchup
2 tablespoons dry sherry
1 1/2 teaspoons fresh lime juice

For the marinade, whisk the lemon juice, olive oil, salt, pepper and thyme in a deep dish. Add the chicken. Marinate, covered, in the refrigerator for 6 hours to overnight.

For the satay, combine the olive oil, sesame oil, onion, garlic, gingerroot and red pepper flakes in a small heavy saucepan. Cook over medium heat for 10 to 15 minutes, or until the onion is translucent. Whisk in the vinegar, brown sugar, soy sauce, peanut butter, ketchup, sherry and lime juice. Cook for 1 minute. Let stand until cool.

Remove the chicken from the marinade, discarding the remaining marinade. Grill the chicken until cooked through. Cut the warm chicken into 1/2-inch strips. Thread the chicken onto skewers and dip in the satay.

Makes 4 servings

Coconut Shrimp

14 medium shrimp
Caribbean Marinade (below)
1 cup sweetened coconut
1/2 cup bread crumbs
1 cup flour
4 cups vegetable oil

Clean, peel and devein the shrimp, leaving the tails on. Place in a shallow bowl. Pour the Caribbean Marinade over the shrimp. Marinate, covered, in the refrigerator for 4 hours.

Mix the coconut and bread crumbs in a shallow dish. Drain the shrimp, reserving the marinade. Coat the shrimp in the flour and shake off any excess. Dip the shrimp in the reserved marinade and coat with the coconut mixture.

Heat the vegetable oil to 350 degrees in a deep fryer or electric skillet. Add the shrimp and deep-fry until golden brown. Serve warm.

Makes 7 servings

Caribbean Marinade

1/2 cup coconut milk
1/2 cup pineapple juice
Juice of 1 lime
1 garlic clove
1/2 teaspoon pepper
2 teaspoons Caribbean jerk seasoning

Combine the coconut milk, pineapple juice, lime juice, garlic, pepper and jerk seasoning in a bowl and mix well.

Makes about 1 1/4 cups

Golden Apple Salad

2 medium Golden Delicious apples
1 (13-ounce) can pineapple tidbits
2 medium carrots, shredded
3 ounces cream cheese, softened
1 1/2 teaspoons grated lemon zest
2 tablespoons lemon juice
2 teaspoons sugar
1/4 teaspoon nutmeg
1/4 teaspoon salt
6 cups crisp salad greens
Salted cashews or peanuts

Core the unpeeled apples and cut into 1/2-inch cubes. Drain the pineapple,
reserving 1 tablespoon syrup. Combine the apples, pineapple and carrots in a bowl.
Blend together the cream cheese, reserved pineapple syrup, lemon zest, lemon juice,
sugar, nutmeg and salt. Gently stir into the apple mixture.

To serve, place the greens in a salad bowl. Mound the apple mixture on the greens
and sprinkle with nuts.

Note: If desired, add 1 cup chopped cooked chicken to the salad and substitute
1 cup fresh pineapple cubes for the canned. Serve the salad in hollowed-out
pineapple halves, rather than over the salad greens.

Makes 6 to 8 servings

Michigan Cherry and Mixed Green Salad

1/2 cup pine nuts
8 cups mixed salad greens, rinsed and dried
1/2 cup dried Michigan cherries
1 small red onion, thinly sliced
1/4 cup (1 ounce) crumbled bleu cheese
Maple Raspberry Dressing (below)

Place the pine nuts on a cookie sheet and toast at 350 degrees for 8 minutes or just until the pine nuts begin to turn brown. Remove from the cookie sheet and cool. Place the greens in a large salad bowl. Add the cherries, pine nuts, onion slices and bleu cheese. Pour 1 cup of the dressing over the salad. Toss and serve.

Makes 8 servings

Maple Raspberry Dressing

1/2 cup olive oil
1/2 cup vegetable oil
1/2 cup maple syrup
1/2 cup raspberry wine vinegar
1 tablespoon Dijon mustard
1 tablespoon dried tarragon

Stir together the olive oil, vegetable oil, maple syrup and vinegar in a bowl. Whisk in the Dijon mustard and tarragon. This dressing may be prepared 1 day ahead and stored in the refrigerator.

Makes 2 cups

Strawberry and Onion Salad

8 cups mixed Bibb lettuce and red leaf lettuce
1 pint fresh strawberries, sliced
1 Bermuda onion, sliced
Poppy Seed Dressing (below)

Rinse the lettuce and pat dry. Chill until serving time. Arrange the greens on individual salad plates. Top each salad with the strawberry and onion slices. Drizzle with the Poppy Seed Dressing. This salad can be prepared in a large bowl instead; toss the greens, strawberries, onion and dressing together.

Makes 8 servings

Poppy Seed Dressing

1/2 cup mayonnaise
2 tablespoons vinegar
1/3 cup sugar
1/4 cup milk
2 tablespoons poppy seeds

Combine the mayonnaise, vinegar, sugar, milk and poppy seeds in a jar with a tight-fitting lid. Close the jar and shake until blended. Will keep in the refrigerator for several days.

Makes about 1 cup

Green Bean Sunshine Salad

The "thumb" portion of Michigan is the bean capital of the world.

2 quarts water
2 pounds small fresh green beans, ends trimmed
4 ounces feta cheese, in small cubes or crumbled
2 hard-cooked eggs, finely chopped
1/2 cup walnuts, toasted
Shallot Vinaigrette (below)

Bring 2 quarts water to a boil in a large saucepan. Add the green beans and cook 4 to 6 minutes, until the beans are tender-crisp. Drain the beans and rinse under cold water to stop cooking. Drain the beans well. Arrange the beans around the edge of a large serving platter like flower petals. Sprinkle the cheese and eggs alternately to form a circle inside the green beans. Cover and refrigerate. When ready to serve the salad, sprinkle the walnuts over the green beans and drizzle with vinaigrette.

Makes 8 servings

Shallot Vinaigrette

3 tablespoons rice wine vinegar
1/4 teaspoon seasoning salt
1/4 cup corn oil
1 tablespoon minced shallots

Place the vinegar and salt in a container with a tight-fitting lid. Shake briefly to mix. Add the corn oil and shallots and shake again. Refrigerate until serving time.

Makes about 1/2 cup

Warm Prosciutto and Parmesan Salad

Dressing
2/3 cup olive oil
8 garlic cloves, thinly sliced
6 tablespoons red wine vinegar
3 tablespoons balsamic vinegar
1/4 cup packed brown sugar

Salad
2 heads red leaf lettuce
1 small red onion, thinly sliced
1/4 cup pine nuts
2 ounces shaved prosciutto, cut into small pieces
1 wedge Parmesan cheese

For the dressing, heat the olive oil in a small skillet over low heat. Add the garlic and cook just until it starts to turn golden brown. Allow the oil to cool slightly. Stir in the red wine vinegar, balsamic vinegar and brown sugar, mixing until the brown sugar dissolves.

For the salad, separate the lettuce heads into leaves. Rinse and pat dry. Tear into bite-size pieces and place in a salad bowl. Top with the onion, pine nuts and prosciutto. Run a vegetable peeler over the surface of the wedge of Parmesan to form about 1/2 cup shavings. Sprinkle over the salad. Pour warm dressing over the salad. Toss gently and serve immediately.

Makes 4 servings

Wilted Red Cabbage Salad

1/2 cup olive oil
2 medium red onions, thinly sliced
4 garlic cloves, crushed
1 tablespoon dried thyme
1 tablespoon fennel seeds
1/4 teaspoon salt
1/8 teaspoon freshly ground pepper

1/3 cup apple cider vinegar
1 medium head red cabbage, cored and
    thinly sliced
1 tablespoon sugar
1/2 cup chopped fresh parsley
2 ounces feta cheese, crumbled

Heat the olive oil in a large saucepan. Add the onions and sauté over medium heat 10 minutes, or until limp. Add the garlic, thyme, fennel seeds, salt, pepper and vinegar. Add the cabbage. Sprinkle on the sugar and cook over medium-low heat until the cabbage wilts, stirring constantly. Cool to room temperature. Sprinkle with the parsley. Add the cheese just before serving so the cabbage doesn't dye it red.

Makes 6 servings

Caesar Salad

2 garlic cloves, crushed
1 1/2 teaspoons Dijon mustard
2 teaspoons anchovy paste
1/8 teaspoon Tabasco sauce
1/4 teaspoon Worcestershire sauce

Juice of 1 lemon
Freshly ground pepper to taste
1/2 cup olive oil
8 cups torn romaine lettuce
1 cup (about) croutons

Place the garlic, Dijon mustard, anchovy paste, Tabasco sauce, Worcestershire sauce, lemon juice, pepper and olive oil in a cruet. Shake well. Place the romaine lettuce and croutons in a salad bowl. Pour on the Caesar dressing and toss gently but well.

Makes 8 servings

Green Salad with Onion Dressing

14 cups torn salad greens
1 cup toasted chopped walnuts
1/2 cup thinly sliced red onion
Onion Dressing (below)

Combine the greens, walnuts, red onion and onion dressing in a large bowl.
Toss well.

Makes 8 servings

Onion Dressing

1 large onion, cut into 8 wedges
1 tablespoon olive oil
1 1/2 teaspoons sugar
1/4 cup chicken broth
2 tablespoons apple cider vinegar
1/4 teaspoon salt
7 tablespoons olive oil

Place the onion wedges in a baking dish. Drizzle with 1 tablespoon olive oil and
sprinkle with the sugar. Bake at 400 degrees for 30 minutes. Turn the wedges over
and bake another 25 to 30 minutes, stirring occasionally, until the onion is tender
and lightly browned. Cool 30 minutes. Place the onion in a blender. Add the
chicken broth, vinegar, salt and 7 tablespoons olive oil. Cover and blend until the
mixture is smooth. It will be thick. Chill until serving time.

Makes about 1 1/4 cups

Caprese Salad

6 to 8 plum tomatoes
1 pound fresh mozzarella cheese
20 to 24 large basil leaves, rinsed and patted dry
3/4 to 1 teaspoon fine sea salt
Freshly ground pepper to taste
Extra-virgin olive oil
Balsamic vinegar

Slice the tomatoes and cheese 1/4- to 1/2-inch thick. Arrange the tomatoes, cheese and basil leaves in an alternating pattern on a large serving platter. Sprinkle on salt and pepper. Drizzle on the olive oil and vinegar. Serve at room temperature.

Makes 6 servings

Mediterranean Rice Salad

5 tablespoons red wine vinegar
2 tablespoons olive oil
1/4 teaspoon freshly ground pepper
1 garlic clove, minced
3 cups cooked rice, warm or at room temperature
1/2 cup diced roasted red bell pepper
1/4 cup halved and pitted kalamata olives
1 (14-ounce) can artichoke hearts, drained and cut into quarters
1/4 cup chopped fresh chives
1/4 cup chopped fresh basil
1/4 cup chopped fresh oregano

Whisk together the vinegar, olive oil, pepper and garlic in a small bowl. Set aside. Combine the cooked rice, bell pepper, olives, artichoke hearts, chives, basil and oregano in a large bowl. Pour on the dressing and toss gently to coat.

Makes 4 to 6 servings

Spinach Salad

$1/2$ pound fresh spinach leaves
1 pint strawberries, rinsed, hulled and halved
4 ounces Gouda cheese, cut into $1/2$-inch cubes
$1/2$ cup coarsely chopped walnuts, toasted
Orange Dressing (below)

Combine the spinach leaves, strawberries and cheese in a large salad bowl. Just before serving, sprinkle on the walnuts and add the dressing. Toss gently to coat.

Makes 6 servings

Orange Dressing

$1/2$ cup orange juice
3 tablespoons vegetable oil
1 tablespoon honey
1 teaspoon grated orange zest
$1/2$ teaspoon poppy seeds
$1/4$ teaspoon garlic salt
$1/8$ teaspoon paprika
$1/8$ teaspoon freshly ground pepper, or to taste

Combine the orange juice, vegetable oil, honey, orange zest, poppy seeds, garlic salt, paprika and pepper in a bowl. Whisk well.

Makes about $3/4$ cup

Kyoto Beef Salad

1 pound filet mignon
2 teaspoons brown sugar
2 cups teriyaki-flavored marinade
12 to 14 ounces fresh spinach leaves
8 to 10 ounces watercress
2 to 3 heads butterhead lettuce

3/4 cup sliced mushrooms
1 garlic clove, crushed
2 tablespoons vegetable oil
1 cup sesame seeds, toasted
3/4 cup chopped scallions
Raspberry Walnut Dressing (below)

Slice the beef into strips 1/2-inch wide and 2 inches long. Stir together the brown sugar and teriyaki marinade in a medium bowl. Add the beef strips and toss to coat. Cover and refrigerate 24 hours, turning occasionally.

Rinse and dry the spinach, watercress and lettuce. Tear into bite-size pieces. Place in a large salad bowl and add the mushrooms.

Heat the garlic in the vegetable oil in a large heavy-bottomed skillet for 1 to 2 minutes, but don't burn. Discard the garlic. Remove the beef from the marinade and drain well; discard the remaining marinade. Add half the beef strips at a time to the skillet and brown about 30 seconds per side for rare, longer for well-done, over high heat. Remove the beef when done.

To serve, arrange the warm beef strips over the salad. Sprinkle with the sesame seeds and scallions. Drizzle part of the dressing over the salad.

Note: For an attractive presentation, form nests for the beef by arranging concentric circles of the salad greens. Cover the serving plate with spinach. Next add a lighter ring of the butterhead lettuce, then the watercress.

Makes 4 servings

Raspberry Walnut Dressing

10 tablespoons walnut oil
2 tablespoons raspberry vinegar
1 tablespoon white wine vinegar

1/4 cup mayonnaise
3 tablespoons honey
Salt and pepper to taste

Whisk together the walnut oil, raspberry vinegar, white wine vinegar, mayonnaise and honey in a bowl. Season with salt and pepper.

Makes 1 1/4 cups

Chinese Chicken Salad

8 to 10 ounces extra-thin egg noodles
1 cup napa cabbage, cut crosswise into
    thin strips
3 whole chicken breasts, cooked and
    shredded into 1/2-inch strips

1/4 cup finely chopped red or green
    bell pepper
1/4 cup chopped fresh parsley
1/4 cup sesame seeds, toasted
Peanut Sauce (below)

Cook the noodles according to package directions and drain well. Spread on a large platter. Sprinkle with the cabbage. Arrange the chicken strips over the noodles and cabbage. Sprinkle on the bell pepper, parsley and sesame seeds. Just before serving, pour the peanut sauce over the salad. The salad and the sauce can both be prepared ahead, covered and refrigerated.

Makes 6 servings

Peanut Sauce

1 tablespoon peanut oil
1 tablespoon sesame oil
1/4 cup chopped scallions
2 dried chiles, including seeds, torn
    into small pieces
1 tablespoon minced gingerroot
2 teaspoons minced garlic

1/4 teaspoon black pepper
1/4 teaspoon cayenne pepper
6 tablespoons soy sauce
1/4 cup red wine vinegar
2 tablespoons sugar
2 tablespoons peanut butter

Combine the peanut oil and sesame oil in a small saucepan and heat slowly. Mix the scallions, chiles, gingerroot, garlic, black pepper and cayenne pepper in a small bowl. Carefully pour into the hot oil and brown slightly.

Combine the soy sauce, red wine vinegar, sugar and peanut butter in a blender. Add the soy mixture to the hot oil mixture and cook, stirring, until the mixture begins to foam. Remove from the heat.

Makes about 1 1/2 cups

Chicken and Rice Asparagus Salad

2 cups cooked rice
3 chicken breasts, cooked and chopped
1 pound asparagus, cooked and cut into bite-size pieces
Chopped scallions to taste
1 cup slivered almonds, toasted
1 cup dried cherries
Honey Dijon Salad Dressing (below)

Place the rice in a large salad bowl. Add the chicken, asparagus, scallions, slivered almonds and cherries. Spoon the dressing over the salad. Toss well and serve.

Makes 4 to 6 servings

Honey Dijon Salad Dressing

1/4 cup mayonnaise
1 tablespoon Dijon mustard
1 tablespoon honey
1 1/2 teaspoons fresh lemon juice

Mix the mayonnaise, Dijon mustard, honey and lemon juice together in a bowl.

Makes about 6 tablespoons

Hot Chicken Salad

4 cups chopped cooked chicken (about 8 breasts)
1/2 cup slivered almonds, toasted
2 tablespoons grated onion
1 (5-ounce) can water chestnuts, drained and sliced
2 tablespoons fresh lemon juice
1 teaspoon salt
1/4 teaspoon pepper
1 teaspoon poultry seasoning
1/4 teaspoon Tabasco sauce, or to taste
1 cup mayonnaise
1/4 cup milk
1 cup (4 ounces) shredded Cheddar cheese
1 can chow mein noodles

Combine the chicken, almonds, onion and water chestnuts in a bowl. Stir together the lemon juice, salt, pepper, poultry seasoning, Tabasco sauce, mayonnaise and milk in a small bowl. Stir into the chicken mixture. Spoon into a greased shallow baking dish. Sprinkle with the cheese and noodles. Bake at 350 degrees for 15 minutes, or until the cheese melts and the mixture is hot. Serve hot.

Makes 6 to 8 servings

Satisfying Salad

Salad
6 cups mixed salad greens
1 cup dried cherries
1/4 cup pine nuts
1/2 cup (2 ounces) goat cheese
2 cups chopped smoked turkey

Dressing
1/2 cup olive oil
1 1/2 tablespoons balsamic vinegar
1 1/2 teaspoons fresh lemon juice
1 small shallot, minced

For the salad, arrange 1 1/2 cups salad greens on each of 4 plates. Top each plate with 1/4 cup dried cherries, 1 tablespoon pine nuts, 2 tablespoons goat cheese and 1/2 cup turkey.

For the dressing, combine the olive oil, vinegar, lemon juice and shallot in a covered container. Shake well. Spoon over each salad.

Makes 4 servings

Chicken Caesar Pasta Salad

2 cups shredded or chopped cooked chicken
3 cups cooked penne
2 cups thinly sliced romaine lettuce
1 1/2 cups halved cherry or grape tomatoes
1/2 cup thinly sliced fresh basil
1/2 cup chopped green onions
1/3 cup fat-free Caesar salad dressing
1/4 cup chopped fresh parsley
4 ounces feta cheese, crumbled
1 garlic clove, minced

Combine the chicken, penne, lettuce, tomatoes, basil, green onions, salad
dressing, parsley, cheese and garlic in a large salad bowl. Toss well to mix and
serve immediately.

Makes 4 servings

Cold Pasta Salad

1 pound rotini (spiral pasta), cooked
Sherry Pasta Sauce (below)
1 small zucchini
4 or 5 mushrooms, thinly sliced
1/2 large red bell pepper, sliced 1/4-inch thick
1 cup sugar snap peas
8 cherry tomatoes, halved
1 avocado, pitted and sliced into thin wedges
1/2 cup blanched whole almonds, toasted
1/2 cup (2 ounces) shredded Gouda cheese

Place the cooked pasta in a large salad bowl. Add the pasta sauce and toss to mix.
Trim and dice the zucchini and add to the pasta. Add the mushrooms, bell pepper,
peas, tomatoes and avocado. Sprinkle with the almonds and cheese. Serve cool,
but not cold.

Makes 8 side-dish or 4 main-course servings

Sherry Pasta Sauce

1 cup semi-dry sherry
1/2 cup vegetable oil
1 garlic clove, chopped
1/2 onion, chopped
1 teaspoon salt
1/2 teaspoon hot red pepper sauce, or to taste
1 cup mayonnaise
2 to 3 tablespoons white wine vinegar

Combine the sherry, vegetable oil, garlic, onion, salt and hot sauce in a small
saucepan. Boil 2 to 3 minutes. Reduce the heat to low and simmer 10 minutes.
Strain and discard the garlic and onion. Spoon the mayonnaise into a bowl.
Slowly whisk in the sherry mixture. Add the vinegar and whisk again.

Makes about 2 1/2 cups

Butternut Squash and Creamy Cider Soup

2 large butternut squash	1 teaspoon thyme
6 tablespoons butter	1/2 teaspoon sage
1 large white onion, diced	5 cups canned chicken broth
1 garlic clove, chopped	1 cup apple cider
3 large carrots, peeled and chopped	1 cup half-and-half
3 Granny Smith or other tart apples	Creamy Cider Topping (below)

Peel and halve the squash. Remove the seeds. Cut the squash into 1/2-inch pieces. Melt the butter in a large saucepan. Add the squash, onion, garlic and carrots. Sauté over medium heat for 20 minutes, or until the vegetables are softened.

Meanwhile, peel, core and chop the apples. Add the apples, thyme, sage, chicken broth and cider to the vegetables. Bring the mixture to a boil. Reduce the heat. Cover the mixture and simmer, stirring occasionally, for 30 minutes, or until the apples are soft. Cool slightly.

Transfer the soup, 1 batch at a time, to a food processor and purée. Return the soup to the saucepan. Whisk in the half-and-half. Bring the soup to a simmer, stirring occasionally. To serve, ladle the soup into bowls and top each serving with a dollop of Creamy Cider Topping.

Makes 8 servings

Creamy Cider Topping

1 cup apple cider
1 cup sour cream

Pour the apple cider into a small saucepan. Bring to a boil and cook over high heat, whisking, until the liquid is reduced to 1/2 cup. Remove the cider from the heat. Whisk in the sour cream until the mixture is smooth. Cover and refrigerate the topping until the soup is served.

Makes about 1 1/2 cups

Posole

1 (2- to 3-pound) pork shoulder roast
1 medium onion, diced
3 to 4 garlic cloves, minced
1 (16-ounce) can diced tomatoes
2 (15-ounce) cans hominy
2 (4-ounce) cans diced green chiles

1 to 2 (48-ounce) cans hot and spicy
   vegetable juice cocktail
1 tablespoon cumin
1 teaspoon oregano
1 tablespoon red chili powder
Salt and pepper to taste

Hominy is dried, hulled corn—whole, coarsely broken, or ground into small pieces.

Place the pork roast in a large Dutch oven. Cover the meat with water. Cover the pan and cook over medium-high heat for 1 hour, or until the meat is tender. Remove the roast and allow to cool. Chill the cooking liquid and skim off the fat.

Cut the pork into bite-size pieces. Return to the Dutch oven. Add the onion, garlic, tomatoes, undrained hominy, pork cooking liquid, green chiles, vegetable juice cocktail, cumin, oregano, chili powder, salt and pepper. Simmer until the onion is tender and the soup is hot.

Makes 10 servings

Mexican Chicken Corn Chowder

4 chicken breasts
3 tablespoons butter
1 small onion, chopped
2 garlic cloves, minced
2 cups half-and-half
2 cups (8 ounces) shredded Monterey
   Jack cheese

2 (14-ounce) cans yellow corn
1/2 teaspoon hot sauce
1/4 teaspoon salt
1 teaspoon cumin
2 (4-ounce) cans diced green chiles
2 tablespoons chopped fresh cilantro

Cut the chicken into bite-size pieces. Melt the butter in a Dutch oven over medium-high heat. Add the chicken, onion and garlic and sauté for 10 minutes, stirring occasionally. Stir in the half-and-half. Add the cheese, a handful at a time, allowing each batch to melt before adding more. Stir in the undrained corn, hot sauce, salt, cumin and green chiles. Simmer the soup for 15 minutes, stirring frequently. Just before serving, stir in the cilantro.

Makes 8 servings

Italian Sausage Soup

2 tablespoons olive oil
1 tablespoon vegetable oil
1 large onion, diced
3 celery ribs, diced
1 to 2 garlic cloves, crushed
3 to 5 links Italian sausage, chopped
4 cups (or more) chicken broth
4 cups (or more) tomato juice
1 (28-ounce) can diced plum tomatoes
1 (16-ounce) can chick-peas, drained
2 tablespoons brown sugar
1 teaspoon marjoram
1/4 teaspoon fennel seeds
1 bay leaf
Salt and pepper to taste
1 (1-pound) box tubetti pasta, cooked and drained
3 tablespoons chopped fresh Italian parsley
Grated Parmesan cheese

Heat the olive oil and vegetable oil in a stockpot. Add the diced onion, celery and garlic and sauté over low heat until the vegetables are tender and translucent but not brown. Add the sausage and brown until it is cooked through. Add the chicken broth, tomato juice, plum tomatoes and chick-peas. Bring the mixture to a boil. Reduce the heat to low. Add the brown sugar, marjoram, fennel seeds and bay leaf. Simmer the soup, uncovered, for 1 hour, stirring occasionally. Remove the bay leaf. Season with salt and pepper.

To serve, spoon the pasta into soup bowls. Ladle the soup over the pasta. Sprinkle each serving with the parsley and grated Parmesan cheese.

Makes about 12 servings

Tortilla Soup

Homemade Chicken Broth (page 87)
1/4 teaspoon celery salt
1/4 teaspoon oregano
1/2 teaspoon cayenne pepper
1 teaspoon cumin
1 (4-ounce) can diced green chiles
1 (15-ounce) can diced tomatoes
    with garlic
2 (14-ounce) cans chicken broth
3 slices bacon
1 large onion, finely chopped

3 garlic cloves, minced
Cooked chicken (from the homemade
    chicken broth)
2 large carrots
1 bunch cilantro, rinsed and finely
    chopped
1 large zucchini
4 (8-inch) flour tortillas
3 tablespoons (or more) olive oil
8 ounces Monterey Jack cheese,
    shredded

Pour the homemade chicken broth into a large stockpot. Add the celery salt, oregano, cayenne pepper, cumin, green chiles, canned tomatoes and chicken broth. Heat over low heat.

Fry the bacon in a medium skillet until crisp. Remove the bacon. Discard the excess bacon drippings in the skillet. Crumble the bacon and return to the skillet. Add the onion and garlic and sauté until tender. Add the chicken. Add the chicken mixture to the chicken broth mixture. Bring the soup to a boil.

Cut the carrots lengthwise into quarters, slice 1/2-inch thick and add to the soup. Cook 15 minutes. Add the cilantro. Cut the zucchini lengthwise into quarters. Slice 1/2-inch thick and add to the soup. Simmer the soup 5 minutes, or until the zucchini is tender.

Cut the tortillas into small pieces. Heat 3 tablespoons olive oil in a medium skillet. Add the tortilla pieces to the skillet and cook over medium heat, turning constantly until the tortilla pieces are golden brown. Add more olive oil if necessary or spray the tortilla pieces with olive-oil-flavored cooking spray. Remove the browned tortilla pieces with a slotted spoon.

To serve the soup, ladle into bowls. Top each serving with 2 to 3 tablespoons of tortilla pieces and 2 to 3 tablespoons cheese.

Note: You can substitute canned chicken broth for the homemade recipe. Add some cooked chicken to the canned broth.

Makes 12 servings

Homemade Chicken Broth

1 (3^{1}/$_{2}$- to 4-pound) chicken, cut up
1 medium onion, coarsely chopped
2 garlic cloves, coarsely chopped
1 medium carrot, coarsely chopped
1 medium boiling potato, coarsely chopped
1 celery rib, coarsely chopped
2 bay leaves
2 quarts water

Place the chicken in a stockpot. Add the onion, garlic, carrot, potato, celery and bay leaves. Add the water. Bring to a boil. Reduce the heat to low. Cover the pan and simmer for 1 hour, or until the chicken separates easily from the bone.

Remove the chicken and strain the broth. Discard the vegetables. Place the chicken and broth in separate containers and refrigerate until chilled. Remove the chicken from the bones and cut into bite-size pieces. Skim the fat from the broth.

Makes about 8 cups

Minted Lemonade

1/4 cup fresh mint leaves
4 cups water
1 cup superfine sugar
1 cup fresh lemon juice (about 6 lemons)
Fresh mint sprigs

Combine the mint leaves, water, sugar and lemon juice in a 2-quart pitcher or jug; mix well. Strain out the mint leaves. Serve over ice and garnish with mint sprigs.

Makes 6 cups

Irresistible Cranberry Iced Tea

2 1/2 quarts water
1 (32-ounce) bottle cranberry juice
1/4 cup fresh lemon juice
2 cups sugar
4 cinnamon sticks
1 tablespoon cloves, tied in cheesecloth
6 tea bags
1 cup orange juice

Combine the water, cranberry juice, lemon juice, sugar, cinnamon sticks and cloves in a 5-quart stockpot. Bring to a boil. Reduce the heat and simmer for 10 minutes. Remove from the heat and add the tea bags. Cover the stockpot for 10 minutes to steep. Remove and discard the cinnamon sticks, cloves and tea bags. Stir in the orange juice. Chill and serve over ice.

Makes 4 quarts

Champagne Punch

2 (46-ounce) cans pineapple juice, chilled
1 (16-ounce) can frozen orange juice concentrate, thawed
2 cups ice-cold water
1/2 cup bottled lemon juice
1 (1-liter) bottle club soda, chilled
2 (750-milliliter) bottles Champagne, chilled
1/2 (750-milliliter) bottle dark rum, chilled
Frozen pineapple slices

Combine the pineapple juice, orange juice concentrate, water, lemon juice, club soda, Champagne and rum in a large punch bowl. Garnish with frozen pineapple slices. For a sweeter punch, dissolve 1/2 to 1 cup sugar in 1 cup hot water. Chill the sugar water before stirring it into the punch.

Makes 50 servings

Cold Coffee Punch

1/2 gallon vanilla ice cream
1/2 gallon chocolate ice cream
1 gallon strong brewed coffee, chilled
1/2 teaspoon almond extract
1 pint whipping cream, whipped
Nutmeg

Place all the ice cream in a large punch bowl. Break up into pieces. Pour the coffee over the ice cream and add the almond extract. Stir until mixed. Top with the whipped cream. Sprinkle lightly with the nutmeg.

Makes 32 servings

Brandy Slush

7 cups water
2 cups sugar
2 cups water
4 tea bags
1 (12-ounce) can frozen orange juice
  concentrate, thawed

1 (12-ounce) can frozen lemonade
  concentrate, thawed
1 pint brandy
1 (2-liter) bottle lemon-lime soda

Combine 7 cups water and the sugar in a medium stockpot. Bring to a boil and cook over medium-high heat until the sugar dissolves. Remove from the heat and refrigerate until cold.

Combine 2 cups water and the tea bags in a saucepan. Boil together for 1 minute. Remove from the heat and let the tea steep 10 minutes. Discard the tea bags. Refrigerate the tea until cold.

Mix together the orange juice concentrate and lemonade concentrate in a large container with a lid. Stir in the sugar-water mixture and tea. Add the brandy. Cover and freeze at least 24 hours, stirring occasionally. To serve, fill tall glasses 3/4 full with the brandy slush. Add the soda to fill. Serve immediately.

Makes about 20 servings

Cosmopolitan

Ice cubes
2 ounces lemon-flavored vodka
1 to 2 ounces Cointreau or other
  orange-flavored liqueur

1 lime, halved
Cranberry juice
Sugar

Place enough ice cubes in a small cocktail shaker to half fill. Add th[e]
liqueur, juice of 1/2 lime and a splash of cranberry juice. Shake well.
remaining lime half around the rims of 2 martini glasses. Place the gl[ass]
down on a plate sprinkled with sugar. Turn sugar-rimmed glasses rig[ht]
Strain the drink into the glasses.

Makes 2 servings

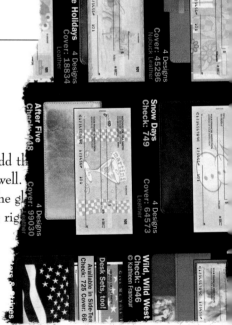

Chocolate Martini

2 ounces chocolate-flavored liqueur
2 ounces vodka
Half-and-half

Combine the chocolate liqueur and vodka in a large glass. Add enough of the half-and-half to turn the drink the color of chocolate milk and stir well. Pour into 2 chilled martini glasses.

Makes 2 servings

Frozen Mango Martini

7 ounces vodka
1 ounce dry vermouth
1/2 cup puréed fresh mango
Ice

Combine the vodka, vermouth and mango purée in a blender. Fill the container half full with ice. Blend until smooth. Immediately strain into 4 chilled martini glasses.

Makes 4 servings

COMPLEMENTS

vegetables

side dishes

JUNIOR LEAGUE OF
BIRMINGHAM, MICHIGAN

Roasted Asparagus with Red Pepper Sauce

3 tablespoons olive oil
2 tablespoons balsamic vinegar
1 tablespoon teriyaki sauce
1 tablespoon dried basil
1/2 teaspoon salt
1/2 teaspoon pepper

1/4 teaspoon dry mustard
1/4 teaspoon nutmeg
1 1/2 pounds fresh asparagus, tough
  ends trimmed off
Red Pepper Sauce (below)

Stir together the olive oil, vinegar, teriyaki sauce, basil, salt, pepper, dry mustard and nutmeg in a 7x11-inch baking dish. Add the asparagus and toss to coat with the teriyaki mixture. Bake the asparagus, uncovered, at 375 degrees for 35 minutes, turning asparagus once. Remove the asparagus with a slotted spoon and serve with Red Pepper Sauce.

Note: If desired, substitute two 10-ounce packages thawed frozen asparagus spears for the fresh.

Makes 6 servings

Michigan ranks third in the nation for asparagus production, growing up to 25 million pounds a year.

Red Pepper Sauce

2 tablespoons olive oil
1 (7-ounce) jar roasted red bell
  peppers, drained and sliced
1/2 small onion, chopped
1 garlic clove, minced
1 tablespoon balsamic vinegar

1 tablespoon orange marmalade
1 tablespoon teriyaki sauce
1/4 teaspoon dry mustard
1/4 teaspoon nutmeg
1/8 teaspoon crushed red pepper flakes
1/4 cup mayonnaise

Heat the olive oil in a large skillet over medium-high heat. Add the bell peppers, onion and garlic and sauté for 2 minutes. Add the vinegar, orange marmalade, teriyaki sauce, dry mustard, nutmeg and crushed red pepper flakes. Cook for 3 minutes. Remove the skillet from the heat and stir in the mayonnaise.

Makes about 1 1/2 cups

Pictured on overleaf: Roasted Asparagus with Red Pepper Sauce (above) and Potatoes Poupon (page 99)

Grilled Asparagus

2 tablespoons water
1 tablespoon lemon juice
2 tablespoons balsamic vinegar
1 tablespoon olive oil
1 teaspoon rosemary
1 teaspoon Italian seasoning
1/2 teaspoon pepper
2 garlic cloves, minced
1 pound asparagus spears, trimmed

Combine the water, lemon juice, balsamic vinegar, olive oil, rosemary, Italian seasoning, pepper and garlic in a bowl and whisk together. Place the asparagus in a large sealable plastic bag. Pour the dressing over the asparagus and turn to coat. Refrigerate the asparagus for 1 to 2 hours before grilling. Remove the asparagus from the marinade; discard the remaining marinade. Place the asparagus on a hot grill. Grill the asparagus to the desired degree of doneness or place the asparagus in a shallow roasting pan and roast at 400 degrees to the desired degree of doneness.

Makes 4 servings

Green Bean and Artichoke Casserole

1/2 cup vegetable oil
1 medium onion, chopped
2 cans French-style green beans, drained
1 can artichoke hearts, drained
1 cup bread crumbs
1/2 cup (2 ounces) freshly grated Parmesan cheese

Heat the vegetable oil in a medium skillet. Add the onion and sauté until tender. Layer the green beans, artichoke hearts, bread crumbs and cheese in a casserole dish. Spoon the onion over the casserole and drizzle with the oil. Bake at 350 degrees for 20 minutes.

Makes 8 to 10 servings

Caramelized Green Beans with Onion

This recipe is easy to make, but it takes a while to cook. Get this dish started before you prepare the rest of the meal.

Onions have been grown since before recorded history. Onions were fed to workers building the pyramids in ancient Egypt and were found in King Tut's tomb.

1/4 cup (1/2 stick) butter
1 large yellow onion, sliced
1/4 teaspoon salt
1/4 teaspoon pepper
1 tablespoon brown sugar
1 pound green beans, rinsed and trimmed

Melt the butter in a large skillet. Add the onion slices and cook over medium heat 10 minutes, or until brown. Do not stir. Sprinkle the onion with the salt, pepper and brown sugar. Reduce the heat to low and continue to cook, stirring frequently, for 30 minutes.

Add the green beans. Increase the heat to medium and cook, stirring frequently, until the green beans are coated with butter and onion. Continue to cook, stirring frequently, for 15 to 20 minutes, or until the green beans are browned and tender.

Makes 4 servings

Dilled Carrots

3 tablespoons butter
2 pounds carrots, peeled and cut into julienne strips
2 teaspoons chopped fresh dillweed, or 1 teaspoon dried dillweed
1/4 cup chicken broth
1 teaspoon honey

Melt the butter in a large skillet over medium heat. Add the carrots and stir well
to coat. Sauté the carrots, stirring frequently, for 3 minutes. Add the dill, chicken
broth and honey. Cover the skillet and cook 5 to 10 minutes, or until the carrots
are tender. Remove the carrots with a slotted spoon and arrange in a serving dish.

Makes 6 to 8 servings

Confetti Vegetables

Salt to taste
1 head of broccoli, florets only
3/4 cup sliced peeled carrots
1/4 cup (1/2 stick) butter or margarine
1 large red bell pepper, diced
2 cups small button mushrooms
1/2 bunch cilantro, coarsely chopped
Pepper to taste

Bring a large saucepan of salted water to a boil. Add the broccoli and carrots
and cook until brightly colored but still crisp and firm. Drain the vegetables in
a colander. Melt the butter in a large skillet. Add the broccoli, carrots, bell pepper,
mushrooms and cilantro. Sauté over medium-high heat until the vegetables are
tender-crisp. Season with salt and pepper.

Makes 6 to 8 servings

Sweet Potato Casserole

Filling
2 pounds sweet potatoes (about 4)
$1/2$ cup packed light brown sugar
$1/2$ cup (1 stick) butter, softened
2 eggs, lightly beaten
$1/3$ cup milk
1 teaspoon vanilla extract

Topping
1 cup chopped pecans
$2/3$ cup packed light brown sugar
$1/2$ cup flour
$1/2$ cup (1 stick) butter, melted

For the filling, peel the sweet potatoes and cut into 1-inch cubes. Place the sweet potatoes in a stockpot with enough water to cover. Bring the water to a boil over high heat. Reduce the heat to medium and cook about 30 minutes, or until the sweet potatoes are tender. Drain well. Place the sweet potatoes in a bowl and mash until smooth. Set aside for 15 minutes to cool. Add the brown sugar, butter, eggs, milk and vanilla. Spread the mixture in a buttered 2-quart baking dish.

For the topping, combine the pecans, brown sugar and flour in a large bowl. Stir in the melted butter. Sprinkle the pecan mixture over the sweet potato mixture. Bake at 350 degrees for 40 to 45 minutes, or until the top is browned and the sweet potato mixture is set in the center.

Note: If desired, you can substitute two 16-ounce cans sweet potatoes for the fresh sweet potatoes.

Makes 6 to 8 servings

What is the difference between a sweet potato and a yam? Although sweet potatoes resemble yams, the tubers aren't related. Yams are large starchy roots indigenous to Africa and are seldom available in the United States. The sweet potato is a native American plant. There are two types of sweet potatoes: one is orange-fleshed, like the yam, and the other is yellow.

Potatoes Poupon

1 tablespoon butter
1/3 cup minced shallots
2 cups heavy cream
1/2 cup Dijon mustard
2 tablespoons butter
1/2 cup (2 ounces) shredded Gruyère cheese
1 tablespoon chopped fresh basil
6 cups thinly sliced peeled potatoes (about 7 or 8 potatoes)
1/2 cup (2 ounces) shredded Gruyère cheese
1/4 cup sliced almonds, toasted (optional)

Melt 1 tablespoon butter in a medium saucepan. Add the shallots and sauté until tender. Stir in the cream, Dijon mustard and 2 tablespoons butter and simmer 5 minutes. Reduce the heat to low. Add 1/2 cup cheese and the basil, stirring until the cheese melts.

Alternate layers of the potatoes and cream sauce in a greased 8-inch-square baking dish. Sprinkle 1/2 cup cheese on top. Bake at 400 degrees for 45 to 60 minutes, or until the potatoes are tender. Let stand for 5 minutes. Top with the almonds.

Makes 8 servings

Spinach Twice-Baked Potatoes

3 large baking potatoes
1/2 cup milk
4 ounces cream cheese, softened
1 cup (4 ounces) shredded sharp Cheddar cheese
1/4 cup finely chopped onion
1/4 teaspoon salt
1/4 teaspoon pepper
1 (10-ounce) package frozen chopped spinach, thawed and drained well
3/4 cup (3 ounces) shredded sharp Cheddar cheese

Bake the potatoes until tender. Cut the potatoes in half lengthwise and scoop out the pulp, leaving the skins intact. Mash the potatoes in a bowl.

Combine the milk and cream cheese in a large bowl, whisking until blended. Add the potatoes, 1 cup Cheddar cheese, onion, salt, pepper and spinach. Stir well. Spoon the mixture into the potato skins. Sprinkle with 3/4 cup Cheddar cheese. Place the stuffed potatoes in a baking pan. Return to the oven and bake at 350 degrees for 15 to 20 minutes.

Makes 6 servings

Garlic Mashed Potatoes

4 to 5 large potatoes, peeled and
   quartered
3 large garlic cloves
1 cup chicken broth

Salt to taste
1/2 cup milk
2 tablespoons butter
Pepper to taste

Place the potatoes, garlic and chicken broth in a large saucepan. Add enough water
to almost cover the potatoes. Season with salt if desired. Bring the water to a boil
and cook until the potatoes are tender. Drain the liquid, keeping the potatoes
and garlic in the saucepan. Add the milk and butter and mash. Season with salt
and pepper.

Makes 6 to 8 servings

Italian Spinach

10 ounces fresh spinach
1 tablespoon olive oil
2 large or 3 small garlic cloves, minced

1/4 cup water
1/4 teaspoon seasoning salt
1/3 cup freshly grated Parmesan cheese

Rinse the spinach thoroughly and remove any large stems. Heat the olive oil in a
large skillet. Add the garlic and sauté for 1 minute over medium heat. Add the
spinach, water and seasoning salt and mix well. Cover the skillet and cook for about
10 minutes, or until the water evaporates and the spinach is tender. Remove from
the heat and sprinkle the cheese over the spinach.

Makes 4 servings

Honey and Brown Sugar Acorn Squash

1/2 cup honey
1/2 cup packed brown sugar
1/2 cup (1 stick) butter, melted
1/2 teaspoon salt
1/4 teaspoon cinnamon
1/4 teaspoon ginger
1/4 teaspoon pumpkin pie spice
4 medium acorn squash

Combine the honey, brown sugar, butter, salt, cinnamon, ginger and pumpkin pie spice in a bowl. Cut the squash lengthwise in half. Remove the seeds and fibers. Spoon the honey mixture into the squash halves. Place the squash in a large greased baking pan and cover with aluminum foil. Bake at 375 degrees for 1 hour. Remove the foil and bake 10 minutes longer.

Makes 8 servings

Honey stays fresh for a remarkably long time. Archaeologists have found honey that was still edible in the tombs of ancient Egyptian pharaohs.

Stuffed Squash Florentine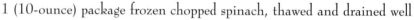

1 (10-ounce) package frozen chopped spinach, thawed and drained well
2 cups (8 ounces) shredded Swiss cheese
13/4 cups light cream
4 eggs, beaten
1 tablespoon butter, softened
1 teaspoon salt
1/8 teaspoon white pepper
1/8 teaspoon nutmeg
4 small Hubbard or acorn squash

Place the spinach in a bowl and add the cheese, light cream, eggs, butter, salt, pepper and nutmeg. Cut the squash in half lengthwise and remove the seeds and fibers. Spoon the spinach mixture into the squash halves. Place in a baking pan and bake at 350 degrees for 30 to 40 minutes, or until the squash are tender and the filling is set.

Makes 8 servings

Corn Pudding

2 tablespoons butter
1 medium onion, finely chopped
1 medium red bell pepper, chopped
4 cups fresh corn kernels
1/4 cup flour
2 cups half-and-half
4 eggs, lightly beaten
1 tablespoon sugar
2 teaspoons Dijon mustard
1 teaspoon salt
1/2 teaspoon baking powder
1/4 teaspoon cayenne pepper

Melt the butter in a large skillet. Add the onion and bell pepper and sauté 5 minutes. Add the corn and sauté 3 minutes longer.

Combine the flour and 1/2 cup of the half-and-half in a bowl and whisk until smooth. Add the remaining 1 1/2 cups half-and-half, eggs, sugar, Dijon mustard, salt, baking powder and cayenne pepper. Add the sautéed corn mixture to the bowl and mix. Pour the corn batter into a buttered 6-cup soufflé dish or baking pan. Place the soufflé dish in a shallow pan. Add enough hot water to the pan to come halfway up the side of the soufflé dish. Bake at 350 degrees for 1 hour.

Makes 8 to 10 servings

Lemon Rice

2¹/2 cups chicken broth
¹/2 teaspoon salt
1 garlic clove, slightly crushed
1 cup rice
1 tablespoon grated lemon zest

2 tablespoons chopped fresh dillweed
  or parsley
2 tablespoons butter, softened
Ground pepper to taste

Bring the chicken broth, salt and garlic to a boil in a heavy saucepan. Stir in the rice. Cover and reduce the heat to low. Simmer 20 to 25 minutes, or until the rice is tender and the liquid is absorbed. Remove from the heat. Stir in the lemon zest and let stand, covered, for 5 minutes. Discard the garlic. Gently stir in the dillweed and butter. Season with pepper.

Makes 4 to 6 servings

Minnesota Rice

¹/4 cup wild rice
1 cup long grain rice
2¹/2 cups water
¹/2 cup beef consommé
1 tablespoon butter

2 cups sliced mushrooms
³/4 cup chopped celery
³/4 cup chopped onion
¹/4 cup dry sherry
¹/4 teaspoon pepper

Rinse the wild rice under hot water. Place the wild rice in a large saucepan. Add the long grain rice, 2¹/2 cups water and consommé and bring to a boil. Cover the saucepan. Reduce the heat and simmer for 1 hour and 10 minutes, or until the rice is tender.

Melt the butter in a large skillet. Add the mushrooms, celery and onion and sauté until tender. Add the mushroom mixture, sherry and pepper to the rice and stir well. Cook the rice over medium heat, uncovered, stirring frequently, until the liquid evaporates. Serve immediately.

Makes 6 servings

Spring Risotto

3 tablespoons olive oil
3 tablespoons butter
8 spears fresh asparagus, trimmed
1 small red bell pepper
1 small onion, diced
2 teaspoons grated lemon zest
2 tablespoons chopped fresh mint
2 tablespoons chopped fresh parsley
2 tablespoons chopped fresh rosemary
$1/2$ teaspoon coriander
$1^1/2$ cups arborio rice
$1/2$ cup dry white wine
$3^1/2$ cups vegetable broth
2 tablespoons fresh lemon juice
$1/3$ cup grated Parmesan cheese
Salt and pepper to taste

Heat the olive oil and butter in a medium heavy-bottomed saucepan. Cut the asparagus into bite-size pieces. Dice the bell pepper. Add the asparagus, bell pepper and onion to the saucepan. Sauté the vegetables until tender.

Mix together the lemon zest, mint, parsley and rosemary in a small bowl. Stir half the herb mixture into the asparagus. Sauté briefly. Stir in the coriander and rice. Cook, stirring frequently, until the rice grains are coated with the oil and butter. Stir in the wine. Reduce the heat to low. Stir in 1 cup vegetable broth. Continue to stir while adding more broth as needed to keep a thin layer of liquid over the rice at all times. Cook the rice mixture 20 to 30 minutes, or until all the broth is used and absorbed and the rice is tender. Stir in the remaining herb mixture, lemon juice and cheese. Season with salt and pepper. Serve immediately.

Makes 4 servings

Orzo with Broccoli, Tomatoes and Feta Cheese

1 to 1¹/2 cups orzo
1 head broccoli, cut into florets
¹/4 cup olive oil
3 tablespoons pine nuts
¹/2 teaspoon crushed red pepper flakes
³/4 cup grape or cherry tomatoes, cut in half
³/4 cup (3 ounces) crumbled feta cheese
³/4 cup kalamata olives, pitted and halved
¹/2 cup (2 ounces) freshly grated Parmesan cheese
¹/4 cup chopped fresh basil
Salt and pepper to taste

Stir the orzo into a large stockpot of boiling water. Cook 8 minutes, or until almost tender. Add the broccoli and cook 2 minutes longer, or until the broccoli is tender-crisp.

While the orzo is cooking, heat the olive oil in a small skillet over medium heat. Add the pine nuts and sauté until golden brown. Add the crushed red pepper flakes and sauté about 30 seconds, or until aromatic. Remove from the heat.

Drain the orzo and broccoli. Transfer to a large bowl. Pour the oil and pine nuts over the orzo and toss to coat. Add the tomatoes, feta cheese, olives, Parmesan cheese and basil. Toss again. Season with salt and pepper. Serve immediately.

Makes 4 servings

Apple Butter

12 apples, peeled and quartered
1 quart sweet apple cider
1^1/2 cups sugar
^{1}/4 teaspoon ground cloves
^{3}/4 teaspoon cinnamon
Toast

Combine the apples and cider in a large stockpot. Cook over low heat, stirring occasionally, until the apples are very soft. Remove the apples from the heat and press through a sieve. Return the apples to the pan. Cook the pulp over low heat until it is thick enough to be scooped with a spoon. Add the sugar, cloves and cinnamon. Cook over low heat for 45 to 60 minutes, or until thick, stirring occasionally. Serve on toast.

Makes about 2 pints

Cranberry Relish

1 (3-ounce) package cherry-flavored gelatin
1 cup hot water
^{3}/4 cup sugar
1 tablespoon lemon juice
1 large can crushed pineapple
1 to 1^1/4 cups ground cranberries
1 orange, peeled and finely chopped
^{3}/4 cup chopped celery
^{1}/2 cup chopped walnuts

Pour the gelatin into a large heatproof bowl. Add the hot water and stir well to dissolve. Stir in the sugar and lemon juice. Drain the pineapple, reserving the syrup. Measure the syrup and add water if necessary to measure 1 cup. Stir the syrup into the gelatin mixture. Chill until the gelatin thickens but is not set. Stir the cranberries, orange, pineapple, celery and walnuts into the gelatin mixture. Chill until firm. This is great with Thanksgiving turkey.

Makes 4 to 6 servings

ENTRÉES

poultry

seafood

meat

pasta

JUNIOR LEAGUE OF
BIRMINGHAM, MICHIGAN

Chicken in Basil Cream

1/4 cup milk
1/4 cup dry bread crumbs
4 boneless skinless chicken breasts
3 tablespoons butter or margarine
1/2 cup chicken broth
1 cup cream
1 (4-ounce) jar sliced pimentos, drained
1/2 cup (2 ounces) grated Parmesan cheese
1/4 cup minced fresh basil
1/8 teaspoon pepper

Place the milk and bread crumbs in separate shallow bowls. Dip the chicken in the milk; then coat with crumbs. Melt the butter in a large skillet over medium-high heat. Add the chicken and sauté about 10 minutes, turning over once, or until the chicken is cooked through. Remove the chicken and keep warm. Add the chicken broth to the skillet. Bring the broth to a boil over medium heat. Scrape the bottom of the skillet with a spoon to loosen the browned bits. Stir in the cream and pimentos. Bring the mixture to a boil and boil, stirring, for 1 minute. Reduce the heat. Add the cheese, basil and pepper. Cook the mixture, stirring, until it is heated through. Pour the basil cream over the chicken.

Makes 4 servings

Basil has a varied and interesting history. In the Hindu religion, basil is revered as a sacred herb. In rural Mexico, people sometimes carry it in their pockets in hopes of attracting money. In the Middle Ages, Europeans thought smelling basil would cause scorpions to form in their brains. They believed scorpions bred where basil grew.

Pictured on overleaf: Maple-Glazed Cornish Game Hens (page 128)

Almond Chicken

3 tablespoons vegetable oil
2 teaspoons salt
2 whole boneless skinless chicken breasts, cut into halves
2 tablespoons soy sauce
1 cup diced celery
1/2 cup diced green bell pepper
1 tablespoon minced onion
1 (4-ounce) can sliced mushrooms
1 (5-ounce) can bamboo shoots, drained
2 chicken bouillon cubes
1 cup boiling water
2 tablespoons cornstarch
2 ounces blanched sliced almonds
Cooked rice

Heat the vegetable oil and salt in a large skillet. Add the chicken and sauté for 5 minutes. Add the soy sauce and mix well. Add the celery, bell pepper, onion, mushrooms and bamboo shoots. Stir the bouillon cubes into the boiling water. Add the chicken bouillon mixture to the skillet. Cover and cook the chicken about 30 minutes, or until cooked through. Combine the cornstarch and a small amount of water in a cup and stir until dissolved. Stir the cornstarch into the skillet. Stir and cook over low heat until the mixture is smooth and slightly thickened. Add the almonds just before serving. Serve over rice.

Makes 4 servings

Chicken with Dried Cherry Sauce

*Michigan produces
70 to 75 percent of
the tart cherries grown
in the United States.
Michigan is the
nation's number one
cherry-producing state.*

1/4 cup flour
1/4 teaspoon salt
4 boneless skinless chicken breasts
1 tablespoon butter
1/2 cup cranberry sauce
1/2 cup ruby port or other sweet red wine
3 tablespoons brown sugar
1/2 teaspoon tarragon
1/4 cup dried tart cherries
1 tablespoon balsamic vinegar
1 tablespoon cornstarch
2 tablespoons water
Cooked rice or noodles

Place the flour and salt in a sealable plastic bag. Add the chicken and shake well
to coat. Place the butter in a large skillet that has been sprayed with nonstick
cooking spray. Melt the butter and add the chicken. Cook for 15 to 20 minutes
over medium heat, turning over once, or until cooked through. Remove the chicken
and keep warm.

Combine the cranberry sauce, port, brown sugar, tarragon, dried cherries and
vinegar in a medium saucepan. Bring the mixture to a boil. Reduce the heat;
cover and simmer for 5 minutes.

Combine the cornstarch and water in a cup and stir well. Stir the cornstarch into
the cranberry mixture. Bring to a boil and cook for 1 minute, stirring constantly.
Serve the chicken over rice or noodles with the sauce.

Makes 4 servings

Chicken Breasts with Vermouth

2 whole boneless chicken breasts
1/4 cup flour
1 teaspoon sage
3 tablespoons unsalted butter
1 cup dry vermouth
2 tablespoons fresh lemon juice
Salt and pepper to taste
Grated zest of 1 lemon

Trim any visible fat from the chicken. Place the chicken between 2 sheets of waxed paper. Flatten the chicken slightly and evenly using a rolling pin. Mix the flour and sage together on a plate. Dust the chicken lightly with the flour mixture and shake off the excess.

Melt the butter in a large skillet over medium heat. Add the chicken and sauté 2 to 3 minutes on each side, or until golden brown and cooked through. Transfer the chicken to a platter and keep warm.

Pour the vermouth into the skillet and bring to a boil over high heat. Scrape the bottom of the skillet with a spoon to loosen the browned bits. Boil the vermouth 2 to 3 minutes, or until the liquid is reduced by half. Add the lemon juice. Season with salt and pepper. Pour the sauce over the chicken and sprinkle with the lemon zest.

Makes 4 servings

Chicken Florentine

1 (10-ounce) package frozen chopped spinach
1 egg, beaten
1 tablespoon grated Parmesan cheese
3/4 cup Italian bread crumbs
3 tablespoons grated Parmesan cheese
4 boneless skinless chicken breasts
Salt and pepper to taste
4 slices Swiss cheese
3 tablespoons butter, melted

Cook the spinach according to the package directions. Drain well and allow the spinach to cool. Combine the spinach, egg and 1 tablespoon Parmesan cheese in a bowl; set aside. Combine the bread crumbs and 3 tablespoons Parmesan cheese in a shallow dish; set aside.

Sprinkle the chicken with salt and pepper. Roll each piece in the bread crumb mixture. Reserve any leftover bread crumbs. Place the chicken in a greased 9-inch-square baking pan. Place a slice of Swiss cheese on top of each chicken piece. Spread the spinach mixture on top of each Swiss cheese slice to form a 1/2-inch-thick layer. Sprinkle on the remaining bread crumbs. Drizzle the melted butter over the chicken. Bake at 350 degrees for 35 to 40 minutes, or until the chicken is cooked through.

Makes 2 to 4 servings

E N T R É E S

Chicken Piccata

1/2 cup flour
1 1/2 teaspoons salt
1/4 teaspoon pepper
6 boneless chicken breasts
1/4 cup (1/2 stick) butter
1/4 cup olive oil
1/4 cup dry white wine or chicken broth
Juice of 1/2 lemon
1/4 cup chopped fresh parsley
Capers to taste

Mix the flour, salt and pepper in a shallow bowl. Place the chicken between 2 sheets of waxed paper and pound to flatten. Roll the chicken in the flour mixture.

Combine the butter and olive oil in a large skillet and heat over medium heat. Add the chicken and sauté 2 to 3 minutes per side. Remove the chicken and drain on paper towels. Keep the chicken warm.

Stir the wine and lemon juice into the skillet and scrape the bottom of the skillet with a spoon to loosen the browned bits. Do not let the mixture come to a boil. Return the chicken to the skillet. Turn the chicken to coat with the sauce. Remove the chicken from the skillet and pour on the skillet juices. Sprinkle on the fresh parsley and capers.

Makes 6 servings

Creamy Chicken Tarragon

4 boneless skinless chicken breasts
Salt and pepper to taste
3 tablespoons butter
2 tablespoons chopped fresh tarragon
3 tablespoons chopped shallots
1/2 cup dry white wine
1 cup heavy cream or half-and-half
2 tablespoons butter
3 tablespoons flour
1/2 cup heavy cream or half-and-half
Cooked wild rice

Season the chicken lightly with salt and pepper. Melt 3 tablespoons butter in a large skillet. Add the chicken and brown on both sides. Sprinkle the chicken with tarragon and shallots. Cover the skillet and cook over low heat for 15 minutes. Sprinkle the chicken with wine; cover and cook 15 minutes longer. Remove the chicken from the skillet and keep warm. Add 1 cup heavy cream to the skillet and stir. Melt 2 tablespoons butter in a small saucepan. Add the flour, stirring constantly. Gradually add the flour mixture to the skillet until the sauce is the desired thickness. Stir in 1/2 cup cream. Top the chicken with the sauce and serve over wild rice.

Makes 4 servings

Grilled Honey Curry Chicken

3/4 cup honey
3/4 cup Dijon mustard
1 1/2 tablespoons curry powder

3 tablespoons soy sauce
6 boneless skinless chicken breasts

Combine the honey, Dijon mustard, curry powder and soy sauce in a medium bowl. Place the chicken in a large sealable plastic bag. Reserve 1/2 cup of the honey-curry mixture. Pour the remaining honey-curry mixture over the chicken. Refrigerate the chicken from 3 to 24 hours.

Remove the chicken and discard the marinade. Grill the chicken until it is cooked through and the juices run clear, basting with the reserved honey-curry mixture. The chicken can instead be baked at 375 degrees for 35 to 45 minutes, or until cooked through.

Makes 6 servings

Grilled Yogurt Chicken

1 cup plain fat-free yogurt
1/4 cup chopped fresh cilantro
2 tablespoons fresh lemon juice
1/2 teaspoon ginger
1/8 teaspoon garlic powder, or to taste
2 teaspoons paprika

1/2 teaspoon coriander
1/4 teaspoon cayenne pepper
1 tablespoon cumin
4 boneless skinless chicken breasts
Cooked rice

Combine the yogurt, cilantro, lemon juice, ginger, garlic powder, paprika, coriander, cayenne pepper and cumin in a large bowl. Add the chicken and coat with the yogurt mixture. Marinate in the refrigerator 1 hour. Grill the chicken until cooked through. Serve the chicken with rice.

Makes 4 servings

Lemon Thyme Chicken

2 tablespoons lemon juice
1 tablespoon brown sugar
1 teaspoon crushed garlic
1/2 teaspoon pepper
1/4 teaspoon salt
1 teaspoon thyme
1/4 cup chicken broth
1 to 1 1/2 pounds chicken breasts
2 medium carrots, sliced
1 pound broccoli, cut into bite-size pieces, or 1 pound broccoli florets
3 tablespoons butter
Cooked rice or noodles

Combine the lemon juice, brown sugar, garlic, pepper, salt, thyme and chicken broth in a small bowl. Place the chicken, carrots and broccoli in a large glass bowl. Pour the marinade over the chicken and vegetables. Cover and refrigerate for 4 hours. Drain well, reserving the marinade.

Melt the butter in a large skillet. Add the chicken and cook 7 to 9 minutes per side, or until the chicken is brown. Reduce the heat. Add the marinade and vegetables to the chicken. Cover the skillet and simmer for 15 to 20 minutes, or until the vegetables are tender and the chicken is cooked through. Serve the chicken and vegetables over rice or noodles.

Makes 4 servings

Among the ancient Egyptians, Greeks, and Romans, thyme was a popular herbal remedy, especially for headache, melancholy, and insomnia.

Lemon Chicken with Artichokes and Capers

2 tablespoons olive oil
1/2 medium onion, sliced
2 garlic cloves, crushed
1 pound boneless skinless chicken breasts, chopped
6 ounces button mushrooms, halved
2 tablespoons flour
1 cup chicken broth
1/4 cup dry white wine or chicken broth
Juice of 1 lemon
Grated zest of 1 lemon
1 (6-ounce) jar marinated or water-packed artichokes, drained and halved
Salt and pepper to taste
Cooked linguini or rice
2 tablespoons capers, or to taste

Heat the olive oil in a large skillet or wok. Add the onion and garlic and cook
3 minutes. Add the chicken and cook until lightly browned. Add the mushrooms
and cook 2 minutes. Add the flour and cook 1 minute, stirring. Remove the
skillet from the heat and gradually add the chicken broth, wine, lemon juice and
lemon zest. Return the skillet to the heat. Bring the mixture to a boil, stirring
until the liquid thickens. Add the artichokes. Cover; reduce the heat and simmer
10 minutes, stirring occasionally, or until the chicken is cooked through. Season
with salt and pepper. Serve the chicken and sauce over linguini or rice and garnish
with the capers.

Makes 4 servings

Lemon Sherry Chicken Supreme

1/4 cup flour
1 teaspoon salt
1 teaspoon paprika
12 boneless skinless chicken breasts
1/4 cup (1/2 stick) butter
1/4 cup water
1 tablespoon cornstarch
2 1/2 cups light cream
1/4 cup sherry
1/2 teaspoon grated lemon zest
1 1/2 tablespoons fresh lemon juice
1 1/2 cups (6 ounces) shredded Swiss cheese
1/2 cup chopped fresh parsley (optional)

Combine the flour, salt and paprika on a plate. Coat the chicken with the flour mixture. Melt the butter in a large skillet. Add the chicken and brown on both sides. Arrange the chicken in a 9x13-inch baking dish. Add the water.

Mix the cornstarch with 1/2 cup of the light cream in a cup. Stir the cornstarch into the pan drippings. Cook over low heat, stirring until smooth. Gradually add the remaining 2 cups light cream, the sherry, lemon zest and lemon juice. Cook, stirring, until the sauce thickens. Pour over the chicken. At this point, the chicken can be refrigerated or frozen.

To cook, cover the dish and bake at 350 degrees for 30 minutes, or until the chicken is cooked through. Uncover the dish and sprinkle with the cheese. Return to the oven and bake until the cheese melts. Top with the parsley.

Makes 10 to 12 servings

Michigan Cherry and Hard Cider Chicken

1 tablespoon butter
1 white onion, chopped
2 garlic cloves, chopped
1 cup flour
$1/8$ teaspoon salt, or to taste
$1/8$ teaspoon pepper, or to taste
8 boneless skinless chicken breasts
3 tablespoons butter
2 tart green apples, peeled and diced
$1^1/2$ cups hard apple cider
1 tablespoon peppercorns
1 teaspoon sage
$1/2$ teaspoon salt
$1/4$ cup dried Michigan cherries

Melt 1 tablespoon butter in a large skillet over medium-high heat. Add the onion and garlic and sauté for 5 minutes, or until lightly browned. Remove the onion and garlic and reserve.

Combine the flour, salt and pepper on a plate. Dredge the chicken in the flour mixture.

Add 3 tablespoons butter to the skillet and melt over medium heat. Increase the heat to medium-high. Add the chicken and cook 6 to 8 minutes, turning once, or until well browned on both sides. Return the onion and garlic to the skillet. Add the apples, cider, peppercorns, sage, $1/2$ teaspoon salt and the cherries. Bring the mixture to a boil. Reduce the heat; cover the skillet and simmer 20 minutes, or until the chicken is cooked through.

Remove the skillet from the heat. Remove the chicken from the skillet and arrange on plates. Carefully strain out and discard the peppercorns. Pour the sauce over the chicken and serve immediately.

Makes 8 servings

Rosemary and Fennel Chicken

Marinade

3 tablespoons lemon juice
1 garlic clove, crushed
3 bay leaves
1/2 teaspoon pepper
3/4 teaspoon salt
3 tablespoons olive oil
6 boneless skinless chicken breasts

Rub

1 teaspoon salt
1 1/4 teaspoons pepper
2 teaspoons rosemary
2 teaspoons large fennel seeds, crushed
Lemon wedges
Rosemary sprigs

For the marinade, combine the lemon juice, garlic, bay leaves, pepper, salt and olive oil in a shallow pan and whisk. Add the chicken and cover with plastic wrap. Refrigerate for 2 to 6 hours, turning the chicken over twice.

For the rub, combine salt, pepper, rosemary and fennel seeds in a cup. Remove the chicken from the marinade and discard the marinade. Rub 1/2 teaspoon of the rosemary mixture on each side of each chicken breast. Grill the chicken until it is cooked through and the juices run clear. Arrange the chicken on a serving platter and garnish with lemon wedges and rosemary sprigs.

Makes 6 servings

Thai Chicken Breasts

2¹/2 tablespoons grated fresh gingerroot
2 tablespoons chopped garlic
¹/8 teaspoon crushed red pepper flakes
4 boneless skinless chicken breasts, pounded thin
¹/2 cup flour
2 tablespoons olive oil
2 tablespoons soy sauce
¹/4 cup packed brown sugar
¹/4 cup white wine vinegar
1 teaspoon fish sauce or anchovy paste (optional)
Cooked Thai rice
1 cup sugar snap peas, rinsed and trimmed

Combine the gingerroot, garlic and red pepper flakes in a cup and set aside. Dredge the chicken in the flour. Heat the olive oil in a large skillet. Arrange the chicken in the skillet and sauté until the chicken is browned on both sides and cooked through. Remove the chicken and set aside; keep warm.

Add the ginger-garlic mixture to the skillet. Sauté until lightly browned. Add the soy sauce, brown sugar, vinegar and fish sauce. Bring the mixture to a boil. Reduce the heat and simmer, stirring frequently, until the sauce reduces and thickens.

Place the chicken on serving plates over Thai rice. Spoon the sauce over the chicken and sprinkle sugar snap peas on top.

Makes 4 servings

Chicken and Spinach Calzones

Filling

1¹/2 cups (6 ounces) shredded Swiss
    cheese
1 cup chopped cooked chicken
¹/4 cup (1 ounce) grated Parmesan
    cheese
¹/2 teaspoon thyme

1 garlic clove, finely chopped
1 small onion, chopped
1 (10-ounce) can cream of chicken
    soup
1 (10-ounce) package frozen chopped
    spinach, thawed and well drained

Calzone Dough

1 package dry yeast
1 cup warm water, 105 to 115 degrees
1 tablespoon sugar
2 tablespoons vegetable oil

1 teaspoon salt
2³/4 to 3¹/4 cups flour
1 egg, beaten

For the filling, combine the Swiss cheese, chicken, Parmesan cheese, thyme, garlic, onion, soup and spinach in a bowl and mix well. Set aside.

For the dough, dissolve the yeast in the warm water in a large bowl. Stir in the sugar, vegetable oil, salt and 1 cup of the flour. Mix in enough of the remaining flour to make an easy-to-handle dough. Turn the dough onto a lightly floured work surface and knead 5 minutes, or until the dough is smooth and elastic. Cover the dough with a bowl and let it rest for 5 minutes.

To assemble, divide the dough into 6 to 8 equal pieces. Roll each piece into a 7-inch circle on a lightly floured surface. Top each dough circle with the chicken mixture, leaving 1 inch of dough around the edge. Fold the dough in half and pinch the edges to seal. Place the calzones on a greased baking sheet. Brush the calzones with the egg. Bake at 375 degrees for 25 to 30 minutes, or until golden brown.

Makes 6 to 8 servings

Chicken Chili

2 tablespoons butter
1/4 cup olive oil
1 cup finely chopped red, yellow or
    orange bell pepper
1 cup chopped yellow onion
4 teaspoons cumin
3 garlic cloves, minced
1 teaspoon chili powder
1 pound chicken breasts, chopped
    (about 3 chicken breasts)
1/2 cup chopped fresh cilantro
1/2 cup dry white wine

1 (12-ounce) can navy beans, drained
1 (28-ounce) can chopped Italian
    tomatoes, drained
1 tablespoon lemon juice
2 tablespoons lime juice
3 cups chicken broth
3 tablespoons cornstarch
3 tablespoons cold water
1/2 cup chopped fresh cilantro
Salt and pepper to taste
Sour cream
Chopped fresh cilantro

Heat the butter and olive oil together in a stockpot. Add the bell pepper and onion and sauté 5 minutes. Add the cumin, garlic, chili powder, chicken and 1/2 cup cilantro. Cook 10 minutes. Add the wine, beans, tomatoes, lemon juice and lime juice. Cook 10 minutes. Add the chicken broth and cook 10 minutes longer.

Combine the cornstarch and cold water in a small bowl and whisk. Add the cornstarch to the chili and stir thoroughly. Cook 5 minutes. Add 1/2 cup cilantro and season with salt and pepper. Ladle the chili into bowls and garnish with a dollop of sour cream and a sprinkling of chopped cilantro.

Makes 6 to 8 servings

Mediterranean Chicken

When purchasing garlic, look for firm, tightly bound cloves. If the garlic has sprouted, discard the bitter green center before using the clove.

2 tablespoons olive oil
1 (3-pound) chicken, cut up
2 garlic cloves, crushed
2 shallots, finely chopped
3/4 cup dry white wine
1 lemon, thinly sliced
4 ounces sun-dried tomatoes, cut into thin strips
12 black olives
1/4 teaspoon pepper

Heat the olive oil in a large skillet over medium heat. Add the chicken and cook 5 minutes per side, or until browned. Add the garlic and shallots and cook 2 minutes. Pour the wine over the chicken. Cover the skillet and reduce the heat; simmer 15 minutes. Add the lemon slices, sun-dried tomatoes, olives and pepper. Cover again and simmer 10 minutes, or until the chicken is tender and cooked through.

Makes 4 servings

King Ranch Chicken

2 teaspoons vegetable oil
2 tomatillos, finely chopped
　(about $1/2$ cup)
1 large onion, chopped
1 garlic clove, minced
2 (4-ounce) jars diced pimentos,
　drained
2 (4-ounce) cans diced green chiles
2 tablespoons finely chopped jalapeño
　chiles
$1/4$ cup ($1/2$ stick) butter
$1/4$ cup flour

4 teaspoons chili powder
1 teaspoon oregano, crushed
$1/4$ teaspoon salt
$1/8$ teaspoon pepper, or to taste
1 (14-ounce) can chicken broth
1 cup sour cream
10 ounces small round flat
　tortilla chips
3 cups shredded cooked chicken
2 cups (8 ounces) shredded Monterey
　Jack cheese

Heat the vegetable oil in a large skillet. Add the tomatillos, onion and garlic and sauté the vegetables until tender. Remove from the heat. Stir in the pimentos, green chiles and jalapeños. Set aside.

Melt the butter in a saucepan. Stir in the flour, chili powder, oregano, salt and pepper. Add the chicken broth. Cook the mixture, stirring frequently, until thick and bubbly. Remove from the heat and stir in the sour cream.

Arrange half the tortilla chips in a 3-quart casserole dish. Layer with half the chicken, half the vegetables, half the sour cream sauce and half the cheese. Add the remaining tortilla chips. Layer with the remaining chicken, vegetables, sauce and cheese. Cover the casserole loosely with aluminum foil. Bake at 350 degrees for 35 minutes. Remove the casserole from the oven and let stand 10 minutes before serving.

Makes 12 servings

Maple-Glazed Cornish Game Hens

It takes about 40 gallons of maple sap to produce a single gallon of maple syrup.

4 Cornish game hens
1/2 lemon
Salt and pepper to taste
Wild Rice and Mushroom Stuffing
   (page 129), or 3 to 4 cups stuffing
   of choice
1/4 cup (1/2 stick) butter, melted

1 cup maple syrup
1/4 cup water (optional)
1 cup dry white wine
1/2 cup heavy cream
2 tablespoons butter, softened
3 tablespoons flour

Rinse the hens under cold water and pat dry. Rub the hens with lemon and season with salt and pepper. Spoon the stuffing into the hens' cavities and truss the birds. Brush the hens with the melted butter. Place on a rack in a shallow roasting pan. Roast at 425 degrees for 10 minutes. Reduce the temperature to 350 degrees and roast for 40 to 50 minutes, basting the hens with maple syrup every 10 minutes. If the pan juices start to burn, add the water and scrape the bottom of the pan. Transfer the hens to a heated serving platter and keep warm.

Pour the pan juices into a bowl and set aside. Set the roasting pan over medium-high heat and add the wine and any remaining maple syrup. Scrape the sides and bottom of the pan with a wooden spoon to loosen the browned bits. Cook the mixture for 5 minutes. Transfer the wine mixture to a medium saucepan. Strain reserved pan juices into the saucepan and bring to a boil. Skim off the fat and simmer for 5 minutes. Add the cream and simmer 5 minutes longer.

Combine the softened butter and flour in a small bowl and stir into the sauce using a whisk. Simmer until the sauce thickens. Season with salt and pepper. Remove the trussing from the hens and serve the hens with the sauce.

Makes 4 servings

Wild Rice and Mushroom Stuffing

1 cup wild rice
3 cups water
1 cup pearl onions
1/4 cup (1/2 stick) butter
1 cup sliced celery
1/2 cup dried mushrooms, soaked in water and sliced
1 teaspoon dried savory
2 tablespoons chopped fresh parsley
Salt and pepper to taste

Rinse the rice; drain and place in a saucepan. Add the water and bring to a boil.
Cover the saucepan and reduce the heat; simmer for 45 minutes. Set aside.

Meanwhile, peel the onions. Trim the tips and roots off the onions. Place the
onions in a heatproof bowl and cover with boiling water. Let stand for 5 minutes.
Drain the onions and cool. Pinch off the skins.

Melt the butter in a skillet. Add the celery, onions and mushrooms and sauté
5 minutes. Remove the skillet from the heat. Add the wild rice, savory and parsley
and mix well. Season with salt and pepper.

This stuffing can be used with the Maple-Glazed Cornish Hens (page 128) or with
other poultry.

Makes 6 to 7 cups

Baked Halibut with Shrimp Sauce

3 tablespoons butter
4 ounces mushrooms, sliced
2 medium tomatoes, peeled, seeded and chopped
1 garlic clove, minced
Salt and freshly ground pepper to taste
6 medium halibut steaks
Shrimp Sauce (below)
1/4 cup (1 ounce) grated Parmesan cheese

Melt the butter in a medium skillet. Add the mushrooms and sauté just until soft. Stir in the tomatoes and garlic. Heat through and season with salt and pepper. Place the halibut steaks in a shallow baking dish. Spoon the tomato sauce over the fish. Bake at 400 degrees for 20 to 30 minutes, or until the fish flakes easily with a fork. Pour the shrimp sauce over the halibut and sprinkle with the Parmesan cheese. Broil the fish until the shrimp topping is bubbly.

Makes 6 servings

Shrimp Sauce

6 tablespoons butter
6 tablespoons flour
1 1/2 cups light cream
1 cup fish stock or clam broth
1/4 cup dry vermouth
1/2 cup (2 ounces) shredded Gruyère cheese
1/4 cup (1 ounce) grated Parmesan cheese
1/2 pound small shrimp, cooked and peeled

Melt the butter until foamy in a medium saucepan. Sprinkle with the flour and cook, stirring, for 3 minutes. Gradually add the cream, fish stock and vermouth. Cook, stirring, until the sauce is well-blended and thickened. Stir in the Gruyère cheese and Parmesan cheese. Cook over low heat until the cheeses melt, stirring frequently. Stir in the shrimp.

Makes about 4 cups

Poached Salmon

1 onion, sliced
1 carrot, sliced
Several sprigs of fresh parsley, snipped
2 garlic cloves, coarsely chopped
1 bay leaf, crumbled
2 peppercorns
2 tablespoons salt
1/2 teaspoon lemon juice or vinegar
1 1/2 pounds salmon, cut into serving-size pieces
Cooked rice
Egg Sauce (below)

Bring a large stockpot of water to a boil. Add the onion, carrot, parsley, garlic, bay leaf, peppercorns, salt and lemon juice. Wrap the salmon in cheesecloth. Ease into the liquid. Reduce the heat to low and simmer 10 minutes per pound of salmon, or until the fish flakes easily with a fork. Remove the salmon. Strain the liquid and reserve the onion and carrot. Serve the salmon over rice and top with Egg Sauce. Serve the cooked vegetables on the side.

Makes 3 or 4 servings

Egg Sauce

1 tablespoon butter
1 tablespoon flour
1/4 teaspoon salt, or to taste
1/8 teaspoon pepper, or to taste
1 cup milk
2 hard-cooked eggs, chopped

Melt the butter in a small saucepan. Add the flour, salt and pepper. Cook over low heat, stirring, until the mixture is smooth and bubbly. Remove from the heat. Stir in the milk. Return the pan to the heat and bring to a boil, stirring constantly until thickened. Boil 1 minute longer. Stir in the eggs and season with salt and pepper.

Makes about 1 cup

Salmon with Ginger and Brown Sugar Glaze

2 tablespoons butter
3 tablespoons light brown sugar
1 1/2 tablespoons honey
1/4 cup Dijon mustard
2 1/2 tablespoons soy sauce
2 tablespoons olive oil
2 tablespoons finely grated fresh gingerroot
8 (6-ounce) salmon fillets
Kosher salt and freshly ground pepper to taste
Olive oil

Melt the butter with the brown sugar and honey in a small saucepan. Remove from the heat and whisk in the Dijon mustard, soy sauce, 2 tablespoons olive oil and the gingerroot.

Season the salmon with salt and pepper and brush with olive oil. Place the salmon, skin-side down, on a heated grill and cook for 10 minutes. Brush the salmon with the glaze. Turn the salmon skin-side up and cook for 6 to 8 minutes. Remove the salmon from the grill and check for doneness. Salmon can be served medium to well-done. Brush the salmon with a final coat of the glaze.

Makes 8 servings

Corn Bread Salmon Bake

1 pound salmon fillets
1 1/2 cups cornmeal
3/4 teaspoon baking soda
1/4 cup finely chopped onion
2 tablespoons chopped green chiles
1 cup buttermilk

2 eggs
1/4 cup vegetable shortening, melted
2 tablespoons prepared mustard
1/4 cup (1/2 stick) butter, melted
1/4 teaspoon Hungarian paprika
Salt and pepper to taste

Cut the salmon into 1x4-inch strips and set aside. Combine the cornmeal, baking soda, onion, green chiles, buttermilk, eggs and shortening in a bowl and stir to mix. Spread the batter in a 7x12-inch baking dish. Place the salmon strips on top of the batter and press into the batter. Paint the top with the mustard and melted butter. Sprinkle on the paprika and season with salt and pepper. Bake at 450 degrees for 20 minutes. If desired, cut the fish and corn bread into rounds or diamonds and serve over beurre blanc sauce as an appetizer course.

Makes 4 servings

Marinated Shrimp Barbecue

1 1/2 pounds medium shrimp
1/2 cup minced fresh dillweed or basil
3 tablespoons olive oil
1 tablespoon minced garlic

1 teaspoon salt
1 teaspoon crushed red pepper flakes
1/4 cup dry white wine

Peel the shrimp and rinse under cold running water. Combine the dillweed, olive oil, garlic, salt and red pepper flakes in a large bowl. Add the shrimp and stir well to cover the shrimp with the marinade. Refrigerate the shrimp 1 hour.

Add the wine to the shrimp 10 minutes before cooking and toss to coat the shrimp. Either grill or broil the shrimp, cooking 1 1/2 to 3 minutes per side, or until the shrimp turn pink.

Makes 6 servings

Shrimp Creole

1 1/2 cups water
1/4 teaspoon salt
1 bay leaf
Juice of 1/4 lemon
1/2 pound fresh shrimp, peeled,
  deveined and rinsed
1 1/2 tablespoons vegetable oil
1 small onion, chopped
1 garlic clove, crushed
1 cup chopped fresh or canned
  tomatoes
1/2 teaspoon sugar
1/2 red or green bell pepper, finely
  chopped

1/2 cup tomato sauce
1/8 teaspoon basil
1/8 teaspoon nutmeg, or to taste
1/8 teaspoon crushed red pepper flakes
1 small piece bay leaf
Salt to taste
2 tablespoons cornstarch
2 tablespoons water
Chopped green onions
Chopped fresh parsley
Cooked rice

Combine 1 1/2 cups water, 1/4 teaspoon salt, the bay leaf, lemon and shrimp in a medium stockpot. Cook the shrimp over medium heat. When the water comes to a boil, cover the pan and cook 5 minutes. Drain, reserving the pan liquids. Set the shrimp aside.

Heat the vegetable oil in the stockpot. Add the onion and garlic and sauté until the vegetables are tender. Do not burn the garlic. Add the tomatoes, reserved shrimp broth, sugar, bell pepper and tomato sauce. Reduce the heat and simmer 15 minutes. Add the basil, nutmeg, red pepper flakes, bay leaf and salt to taste. Cook about 5 minutes.

Combine the cornstarch with 2 tablespoons water in a cup. Stir the cornstarch into the sauce and cook until the sauce thickens. If necessary, add more cornstarch and water mixture. When ready to serve, add the shrimp to the sauce and heat through. Sprinkle with the chopped green onions and parsley. Serve the shrimp over rice.

Makes 2 servings

Portuguese Seafood Stew

1 tablespoon olive oil
1 tablespoon butter
1 onion, chopped
2 to 3 garlic cloves, minced
1 red bell pepper, chopped
1 large can chopped tomatoes
1 cup beef broth
1/2 cup dry white wine
1/2 teaspoon sugar
1/2 teaspoon dried basil, or 1 tablespoon fresh basil
1/8 to 1/4 teaspoon cayenne pepper
1 pound shrimp, peeled and deveined
2 pounds firm fish, such as tilapia, cut into 1-inch cubes
Salt and pepper to taste
3 cups water
1 1/2 cups long grain or brown rice
Cooked green peas

Heat the olive oil and butter in a Dutch oven. Add the onion and garlic and sauté until the vegetables are translucent. Add the bell pepper, tomatoes, beef broth, white wine, sugar, basil and cayenne pepper. Bring the mixture to a boil. Reduce the heat and simmer 15 minutes. Increase the heat to medium. Add the shrimp. Cover and cook about 4 minutes, or until the shrimp turn pink. Add the fish and immerse in the sauce. Cover and cook 3 to 4 minutes, or until the fish is opaque. Season with salt and pepper.

Meanwhile, bring the water to a boil in a medium saucepan. Stir in the rice. Reduce the heat to low. Cover the pan and cook 20 minutes for long grain rice, or 45 to 50 minutes for brown rice. Stir in the peas and heat through. Serve the fish and sauce over the rice.

Makes 4 servings

Spicy Cioppino

1/4 cup olive oil
2 garlic cloves, finely chopped
3/4 cup finely chopped onion
1 teaspoon Italian seasoning
2 cups dry white wine
3 cups fish stock
1/2 pound cleaned and sliced squid or
  bay scallops

1 cup chopped tomatoes
36 large shrimp, peeled
24 clams, scrubbed
18 to 24 mussels, scrubbed and
  beards removed
6 small white fish fillets
Salt and pepper to taste
Thick crusty bread

Heat the olive oil in a large skillet. Add the garlic and onion and sauté until translucent. Add the Italian seasoning, white wine and fish stock. Simmer for 5 minutes. Add the squid and tomatoes and cook for 5 minutes. Add the shrimp, clams and mussels and cook for 3 to 5 minutes. Add the fish fillets to the stew and cook 5 to 8 minutes. Season with salt and pepper. Serve with thick crusty bread.

Makes 6 servings

Thai Coconut Shrimp

1 cup chicken broth
1 cup coconut milk
2 teaspoons Thai chili paste, or to
  taste
1 teaspoon salt
15 jumbo shrimp, peeled and deveined,
  or 1 pound boneless skinless
  chicken breast, chopped
2 medium Roma tomatoes, cored and
  cut into quarters

2 ounces pineapple chunks, or to taste
1 tablespoon lime juice
2 tablespoons lemon juice
2 tablespoons cornstarch
2 tablespoons water
Cooked rice
3 tablespoons chopped green onions,
  or to taste
2 tablespoons chopped fresh cilantro,
  or to taste

Pour the chicken broth into a large stockpot and bring to a boil. Add the coconut milk, chili paste, salt, shrimp, tomatoes, pineapple chunks, lime juice and lemon juice. Mix well. Boil until the shrimp turn pink. Stir together the cornstarch and water in a cup. Stir the cornstarch paste into the shrimp mixture. Bring to a boil again, stirring until the mixture thickens. Add more cornstarch paste for a thicker consistency if desired. Serve the coconut shrimp over rice. Sprinkle with the green onions and cilantro.

Makes 4 servings

Beef Tenderloin with Asparagus and Feta Cheese

4 (4-ounce) beef tenderloin steaks
2 teaspoons chopped fresh thyme
1/4 teaspoon salt
1/4 teaspoon pepper
1 tablespoon butter
1 tablespoon olive oil
1 cup dry white wine
1/2 cup beef consommé
1/2 cup half-and-half
12 small asparagus
1/2 to 3/4 cup (2 to 3 ounces) crumbled feta cheese
Cooked rice

Rub the steaks with thyme, salt and pepper. Melt the butter in a large skillet over medium heat. Add the olive oil. Add the steaks and cook 4 to 6 minutes on each side, or to the desired doneness. Remove the steaks and keep warm. Stir the wine and consommé into the drippings. Increase the heat to high. Stir frequently and reduce the liquid to 1/2 cup. Stir in the half-and-half and cook, stirring constantly, to reduce the liquid to 1/2 cup. Cut the asparagus in half and place in a steamer basket over water. Steam 8 minutes. Place the steaks on a broiler pan. Top the steaks with asparagus and sprinkle with the feta cheese. Broil the steaks 6 inches from the heat for 2 minutes, or until the cheese melts. Serve the wine sauce with the steaks. Serve with rice.

Makes 4 servings

Michigan Pasties

Filling
1/2 cup cubed turnips
1/2 cup cubed potatoes
1/2 cup cubed carrots
2 tablespoons minced fresh or dried
  parsley

1 medium onion, diced
1 pound boneless beef, cubed
1/2 teaspoon salt
1/4 teaspoon pepper
1 tablespoon butter

Crust
1 1/3 cups flour
1/2 teaspoon salt

1/2 cup vegetable shortening
1/3 cup cold water

Accompaniments
Beef gravy
Ketchup

Pickle relish
Chutney

For the filling, combine the turnips, potatoes, carrots, parsley, onion, beef, salt and pepper in a bowl. Set aside.

For the crust, sift the flour and salt into a bowl. Cut in the shortening until the mixture resembles small peas. Gradually add the cold water and mix with a pastry blender until the dough is well blended and comes together. Divide the dough into 2 equal parts.

Roll the dough into 9-inch circles. Spoon half the filling onto half of each rolled crust. Top each filling with half the butter. Lift and fold the top half of the crust over the filling. To seal, fold and crimp the dough into a rope edge along the top of the pasty. Make several 1/2-inch slashes in each pasty. Place the pasties several inches apart on a baking sheet. Bake at 375 degrees for 1 hour. Serve pasties with beef gravy, ketchup, pickle relish or chutney.

Makes 2 servings

The pasty (pronounced pass-tee) is a delicious blend of meat and vegetables baked in a light pie crust. A portable beef stew, the pasty originated as a savory handheld meal for Cornish copper miners, who didn't have the time to come above ground for lunch while working in Michigan's Upper Peninsula. Today, residents of the Upper Peninsula consume thousands of pasties each year.

Spinach-Stuffed Beef Tenderloin

2 tablespoons butter or margarine
6 cups sliced shiitake or button
   mushroom caps
1 cup chopped shallots
1/4 cup brandy
2 teaspoons olive oil
16 cups torn spinach
3 garlic cloves, minced
1/2 teaspoon salt

1/2 teaspoon pepper
1 (4-pound) beef tenderloin, trimmed
   of fat
1/4 teaspoon salt
1/4 teaspoon pepper
1 teaspoon olive oil
1/2 teaspoon salt
1/4 teaspoon pepper

Melt the butter in a large nonstick skillet over medium-high heat. Add the mushrooms and shallots and sauté for 4 minutes. Add the brandy. Cook for 30 seconds, or until the liquid evaporates. Spoon the mixture into a large bowl. Set aside.

Heat 2 teaspoons olive oil in a large saucepan or Dutch oven over medium heat. Add the spinach and garlic and sauté 30 seconds, or until the spinach wilts. Place the spinach mixture in a colander. Press the spinach with the back of a spoon until the spinach is barely moist. Add the spinach mixture, 1/2 teaspoon salt and 1/2 teaspoon pepper to the mushroom mixture. Mix well.

To butterfly the tenderloin, slice lengthwise, cutting to but not through the other side. Open the halves laying the tenderloin flat. Slice each half lengthwise, cutting to but not through the other side; open flat. Cover the tenderloin with plastic wrap. Flatten the meat to 1/4-inch thickness using a meat mallet or a rolling pin. Sprinkle 1/4 teaspoon salt and 1/4 teaspoon pepper over the tenderloin. Spread the spinach mixture down the center of the tenderloin to within 1/2-inch of the sides. Fold over 3 to 4 inches of the small end. Roll up the tenderloin jelly-roll fashion, starting with the long side. Secure the meat at 2-inch intervals using heavy kitchen string. Brush 1 teaspoon olive oil over the tenderloin. Sprinkle with 1/2 teaspoon salt and 1/4 teaspoon pepper. Place the tenderloin on a broiler pan coated with cooking spray. Cover the meat and refrigerate until chilled.

Insert a meat thermometer into the thickest portion of the tenderloin. Bake at 500 degrees for 10 to 15 minutes. Reduce the heat to 425 degrees and continue cooking for 25 to 40 minutes, or until the meat thermometer registers 145 degrees for medium rare or 160 degrees for medium. Let the meat stand for 10 minutes before slicing.

Makes 10 servings

Italian Beef

1 pound eye-of-round roast (rump roast)
3 onions, chopped
1 tablespoon salt
1 1/2 cups water
1 teaspoon crushed garlic
1 teaspoon oregano, crushed
1/2 teaspoon basil
1 teaspoon Italian seasoning
1 1/2 to 2 fresh or canned hot peppers, chopped
Small French rolls

Place the eye-of-round, onions, salt and water in a Dutch oven. Cover and bake at 325 degrees for 2 hours. Remove the roast and cool, reserving the liquid. Slice the beef and place in a large bowl. Add the garlic, oregano, basil and Italian seasoning to the reserved liquid in the Dutch oven. Bring the liquid to a boil. Pour the liquid over the beef. Add the hot peppers. Cover and refrigerate 24 hours.

To serve, reheat the beef in the reserved liquid. Serve the beef on French rolls with au jus dip.

Makes 4 servings

Grant, in the southern lower portion of Michigan, is noted for the onions it grows.

ENTRÉES

Marinated Korean Flank Steak

3 tablespoons sesame seeds
1/2 cup vegetable oil
1/4 cup soy sauce
1 garlic clove, crushed
1/4 teaspoon grated fresh gingerroot
2 teaspoons brown sugar
1 1/2 pounds flank steak

Combine the sesame seeds, vegetable oil, soy sauce, garlic, gingerroot and brown sugar in a large bowl and mix well. Add the flank steak, turning the meat so that both sides are coated with the marinade. Cover the bowl and refrigerate overnight. Remove the flank steak from the marinade, discarding the remaining marinade. Cook the steak on a hot grill to the desired degree of doneness.

Makes 6 servings

St. Patty's Favorite Corned Beef

1 (3- to 4-pound) beef brisket
1 tablespoon pickling spices
1 large carrot, cut into strips
3 celery ribs
1 large orange, cut into thick slices
1/2 cup water
Steamed Cabbage (below)
1/2 cup mayonnaise (optional)
2 tablespoons prepared mustard (optional)

Cabbage is

91 percent water.

Rinse the brisket well under cold water. Place the brisket in a large bowl and fill with cold water. Soak for 20 minutes. Place the brisket on a long sheet of heavy-duty aluminum foil. Sprinkle the pickling spices on the brisket. Lay the carrot strips on top of the meat. Add the celery and the orange slices. Pour the water over the meat. Close the foil to seal tightly. Place the brisket in a baking pan and bake at 350 degrees for 1 hour. Reduce the temperature to 275 degrees and bake for 3 to 4 hours. Remove the beef from the oven. Arrange the meat on a platter. Discard the vegetables and orange slices, but reserve the remaining liquid for steaming the cabbage. If desired, mix the mayonnaise with the mustard and serve as a sauce.

Makes 6 to 8 servings

Steamed Cabbage

3 to 4 cups sliced green cabbage
1 1/2 cups cooking liquid from the corned beef

Place the cabbage and the broth in a saucepan and cover. Simmer the cabbage for 15 minutes, or until tender. Drain and serve.

Makes 6 to 8 servings

Scaloppine alla Marsala

1 1/2 pounds veal scallops, sliced 3/8-inch thick
Salt and freshly ground pepper to taste
Flour
2 tablespoons butter
3 tablespoons olive oil
1/2 cup dry marsala
1/2 cup fresh or canned chicken broth or beef broth
2 tablespoons butter, softened

Pound the veal scallops 1/4-inch thick and season with salt and pepper. Dust the veal with flour and shake off the excess. Melt 2 tablespoons butter with the olive oil in a heavy 10- to 12-inch skillet. When the foam subsides, add the veal, 3 or 4 pieces at a time, and brown for 3 minutes on each side. Remove the veal to a plate.

Discard most of the fat in the skillet, leaving a thin film. Add the wine and 1/4 cup of the chicken broth and boil the liquid briskly over high heat for 1 to 2 minutes. Scrape up any browned bits on the bottom or side of the skillet. Return the veal to the skillet. Cover the skillet and simmer for 10 to 15 minutes, basting the veal occasionally with pan juices.

To serve, remove the veal to a heated platter. Add the remaining 1/4 cup broth to the skillet and bring to a brisk boil, scraping in any browned bits sticking to the bottom and side of the skillet. Reduce the sauce to the consistency of a syrupy glaze. Taste for seasoning. Remove the skillet from the heat. Stir in the softened butter. Pour the sauce over the veal.

Makes 4 servings

Stuffed Cabbage

1 large head cabbage
3 pounds ground chuck
1 pound bulk pork sausage
2 eggs
1 to 2 cups cooked rice
Spanish rice seasoning packet
Salt and pepper to taste
1 (32-ounce) jar sauerkraut
3/4 cup packed brown sugar
1 (32-ounce) can tomato juice

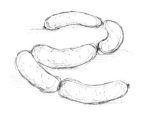

*Cedar, in the northern
lower portion of Michigan,
is the sausage capital
of Michigan.*

Fill a large stockpot with water and bring to a boil. Remove the pan from the heat
and add the cabbage, submerging it in the water. Cover the pan and set aside
1 hour. Remove the cabbage and let cool. Peel off 24 to 30 large leaves.

Combine the ground chuck, pork sausage, eggs, rice and seasoning packet in a large
bowl. Season lightly with salt and pepper. Mix the meat mixture by hand. The meat
should stick together but not be densely packed.

Place one handful of the meat mixture in the bottom center of a cabbage leaf. Fold
the bottom of the leaf over the meat mixture. Fold the left side to the center, then
the right side to the center. Roll up, if necessary, to close the top of the leaf. Secure
the stuffed cabbage with a wooden pick if necessary. Repeat with the remaining
cabbage leaves and filling.

Cover the bottom of a large roasting pan with the sauerkraut. Sprinkle with the
brown sugar. Arrange the stuffed cabbages in the pan. Pour the tomato juice over
the cabbage rolls. Cover the pan. Bake at 325 degrees for 3 to 4 hours.

Makes 24 to 30 servings

Stuffed Green Peppers

3 large or 6 medium green bell peppers
1/2 teaspoon salt
1 tablespoon vegetable oil
1 pound ground beef
1 tablespoon finely chopped onion
1/3 cup chopped celery
1 1/2 cups cooked rice
1 cup tomato paste
1 teaspoon salt
1/4 teaspoon oregano
Tomato sauce (optional)
Grated cheese (optional)

Cut large bell peppers lengthwise in half; cut the tops off medium bell peppers. Rinse the peppers well. Bring a large stockpot of water to a boil with 1/2 teaspoon salt. Add the peppers and simmer in the boiling water 5 minutes. Drain and set aside.

Heat the vegetable oil in a medium skillet. Add the ground beef, onion and celery and cook until the vegetables are soft and the ground beef is lightly browned. Pour off any fat. Stir in the cooked rice, tomato paste, 1 teaspoon salt and the oregano and mix thoroughly. Spoon the ground beef mixture into the peppers. Place the stuffed peppers in a shallow baking pan. Bake at 375 degrees for 20 minutes, or until the peppers are lightly browned. If desired, top each pepper with tomato sauce and a sprinkling of grated cheese before baking.

Makes 6 servings

Lamb Chops with Lemon and Thyme

In ancient Greece, thyme was used as incense and symbolized courage.

1/2 cup Dijon mustard
1/2 cup fresh lemon juice
6 tablespoons balsamic vinegar
3 tablespoons chopped fresh thyme
1 teaspoon pepper
2/3 cup extra-virgin olive oil
24 lamb rib chops or loin chops
Salt to taste
1 lemon, halved

Mix the Dijon mustard, lemon juice, vinegar, thyme and pepper in a medium bowl. Gradually whisk in the olive oil. Divide the marinade between 2 large shallow baking dishes. Arrange 12 lamb chops in each dish, turning to coat with the marinade. Cover and refrigerate the lamb 2 to 4 hours.

Grill the lamb 7 minutes per side for medium-rare or grill to desired doneness. Place the lamb on a serving platter. Season with salt. Squeeze lemon juice over the lamb.

Makes 8 servings

Lamb Kabobs

$^1/_2$ cup dry white wine
$^1/_4$ cup lemon juice
1 tablespoon olive oil
1 garlic clove, pressed
$^1/_2$ teaspoon basil
$^1/_2$ teaspoon oregano
$^1/_4$ teaspoon thyme
1 tablespoon Worcestershire sauce
Salt and pepper to taste
1 pound boneless lamb, cut into $1^1/_2$-inch cubes
6 small white onions
$^1/_2$ pineapple, cut into 8 wedges
4 bay leaves, soaked in water
$^1/_4$ pound mushrooms, stems removed
1 small green bell pepper, cut into quarters
1 small bottle crab apples

Combine the white wine, lemon juice, olive oil, garlic, basil, oregano, thyme, Worcestershire sauce, salt and pepper in a large bowl and stir well. Add the lamb. Refrigerate several hours or overnight. Drain the lamb, reserving the marinade. Pour the marinade into a small saucepan and boil for 2 minutes. Cook the onions in a small saucepan of boiling salted water for 5 minutes. Drain the onions.

Thread the lamb cubes, onions, pineapple wedges, bay leaves, mushrooms, bell pepper and crab apples on 2 long kabob skewers. Grill the kabobs over hot coals for 12 to 16 minutes, brushing frequently with the marinade.

Makes 4 to 6 servings

Grilled Tenderloin Pork

2 tablespoons Szechuan sauce
2 tablespoons orange mandarin sauce
1 tablespoon sesame oil or hot
   sesame oil

2 tablespoons soy sauce
1¹/2 to 2 pounds pork tenderloin

Place Szechuan sauce, orange mandarin sauce, sesame oil and soy sauce in a
resealable plastic bag. Add the pork and turn to coat all sides. Refrigerate the pork
in the marinade up to 2 days, turning occasionally. If desired, freeze the pork in the
marinade and thaw in the refrigerator. Remove the pork and reserve the marinade.

Grill the pork 7 to 10 minutes on each side. Heat the marinade in a small
saucepan and serve as a sauce with the pork.

Makes 4 servings

Breaded Pork Tenderloin

1¹/2 to 2 pounds pork tenderloin
¹/2 cup bread crumbs
3 tablespoons sliced almonds, finely
   chopped
1 tablespoon dried rosemary

1 teaspoon coarsely ground pepper
¹/2 teaspoon salt
2 egg whites, lightly beaten
Fresh rosemary sprigs

Trim the fat from the pork. Combine the bread crumbs, almonds, dried rosemary,
pepper and salt in a shallow pan. Pour the egg whites into a shallow dish. Dip the
pork in the egg whites; then dredge in the bread crumb mixture. Place the pork on
a rack in a baking pan. Bake at 425 degrees for 30 minutes or until the internal
temperature reaches 160 degrees. Remove the pork from the oven. Cover with
aluminum foil and let stand 10 minutes. Garnish the pork with rosemary sprigs.
Serve the pork with Cranberry and Apple Chutney (page 149).

Makes 4 to 6 servings

Cranberry and Apple Chutney

2 cups sweetened dried cranberries
1¹/2 cups boiling water
¹/3 cup diced dried apples
¹/4 cup raisins
1 tablespoon minced crystallized ginger
¹/3 cup white wine vinegar
3 tablespoons sugar
¹/8 teaspoon cayenne pepper
¹/8 teaspoon allspice, or to taste
¹/8 teaspoon cinnamon, or to taste
¹/8 teaspoon ginger, or to taste
¹/4 cup red plum jam or raspberry jam

Combine the cranberries, boiling water, dried apples, raisins and crystallized ginger in a heatproof bowl. Let stand for 30 minutes.

Combine the vinegar, sugar, cayenne pepper, allspice, cinnamon and ginger in a small saucepan. Bring to a boil, stirring frequently. Add the fruit mixture. Bring to a boil. Reduce the heat to low and simmer for 5 minutes. Stir in the jam. Remove the mixture from the heat and cool to room temperature.

Makes 2¹/2 cups

Stuffed Pork Loin

To roast garlic, cut off the top of a garlic bulb to expose the cloves. Place the bulb on a sheet of aluminum foil and drizzle with olive oil. Draw up the foil to completely cover the garlic. Bake at 350 degrees for 30 minutes. Remove the garlic and let cool. Squeeze the garlic cloves out of the skins and mash. For 1/2 cup mashed garlic, use 2 to 3 bulbs.

1 tablespoon olive oil
1/2 Spanish onion, diced
3 tablespoons chopped fresh thyme
1/2 cup mashed roasted garlic (at left)
3/4 cup dry white wine
1 (10-ounce) package frozen spinach, thawed and drained
1 cup grape tomatoes, halved
1 teaspoon kosher salt
1 teaspoon black pepper
1/8 teaspoon cayenne pepper, or to taste
1 tablespoon butter, softened
1 cup (4 ounces) grated Parmesan cheese
3 cups toasted croutons
2 pounds pork loin, butterflied and pounded thin
Salt and pepper to taste

Heat the olive oil in a large skillet. Add the onion and sauté briefly. Add the thyme, garlic, white wine, spinach, tomatoes, salt, 1 teaspoon black pepper and the cayenne pepper and cook briefly. Remove from the heat. Stir the butter, cheese and croutons into the spinach mixture.

Lay the pork flat on a work surface and spread with the spinach mixture. Roll up the pork jelly-roll style and tie with kitchen twine. Place the pork in a 9x13-inch baking pan. Season the pork with salt and pepper to taste. Pour a small amount of water into the pan. Bake at 325 degrees for 1 hour and 15 minutes.

Makes 4 to 6 servings

Balsamic Pork Tenderloin

2 tablespoons butter
2 garlic cloves, finely chopped
1/4 cup dry white wine
1 pork tenderloin
1/4 cup balsamic vinegar
1/4 cup chicken broth
2 tablespoons butter
Salt and pepper to taste

Melt 2 tablespoons butter in a large skillet. Add the garlic and sauté 5 minutes over medium heat. Add the wine and bring to a boil over medium heat. Add the pork to the skillet. Cook the pork 15 to 20 minutes, turning once, or until cooked through. Remove the pork and keep warm.

Combine the vinegar and chicken broth. Pour the liquid into the hot skillet and cook over high heat until the liquid is reduced by half. Add 2 tablespoons butter and whisk until the sauce is glossy.

Slice the pork into cutlets and spoon the balsamic sauce on top. Season with salt and pepper.

Makes 4 servings

Cudighi

Patties

2 1/4 teaspoons salt
3/4 teaspoon black pepper
3/8 teaspoon nutmeg
1/4 teaspoon ground cloves
3/16 teaspoon allspice

1/2 teaspoon garlic powder
1/2 teaspoon cayenne pepper
1/8 teaspoon cinnamon
1/8 teaspoon mace
2 pounds ground pork

Sandwiches

1 onion, sliced
1/2 pound fresh mushrooms, sliced
6 ounces sliced mozzarella cheese

6 ounces (or more) pizza sauce
6 Italian (hoagie) buns

Cudighi is a recipe from Marquette County in Michigan's Upper Peninsula. The meat recipe, Italian in origin, is kept secret by families and restaurateurs. The very special spice combination flavors the meat in an indescribable way.

For the patties, stir the salt, black pepper, nutmeg, cloves, allspice, garlic powder, cayenne pepper, cinnamon and mace together in a large bowl. Add the pork and thoroughly mix the spices into the pork. Cover the pork and refrigerate several hours or overnight.

Shape the pork into large rectangular patties that will fit the buns. Fry in a large skillet until the meat is browned on both sides but still moist.

For the sandwiches, add the onion and mushrooms to the skillet and cook until browned, or brown the vegetables in a separate skillet. Top each pork patty with a slice of cheese. Let the cheese melt. Warm the pizza sauce and spoon it over each patty. Gently transfer the cheese-topped pork patties to the buns. Top each serving with mushrooms and onions and spoon on more sauce if desired.

Makes 6 large servings

Tortière

2 tablespoons butter
1 large onion, finely chopped
2 garlic cloves, minced
2 pounds ground meat, equal parts beef, veal and pork mixed together
3/4 teaspoon salt
3/4 teaspoon pepper
1 teaspoon sage
1/2 teaspoon allspice
1/4 teaspoon ginger
1/4 teaspoon garlic salt
1/2 cup water
2 potatoes, cooked, peeled and diced
2 teaspoons dried parsley
Salt and pepper to taste
1 unbaked double-crust pie pastry, prepared from Basic Pie Crust recipe
   (page 192)

Melt the butter in a large skillet. Add the onion and sauté until translucent. Add the garlic and sauté briefly. Add the meat mixture, salt, pepper, sage, allspice, ginger, garlic salt and water. Mix well. Cover the skillet and cook over medium-low heat for 1 hour, stirring occasionally. Simmer until the meat is cooked through. Drain off the fat. Mix the potatoes and parsley into the meat mixture and season with salt and pepper.

Spoon the meat mixture into a pastry-lined pie plate. Cover the meat mixture with a top pastry. Make several slashes in the top pastry to allow steam to vent. Bake at 350 degrees for 45 minutes, or until the crust is light golden brown.

Makes 6 servings

Basil Venison Tenderloin and Broccoli Stir-Fry

1 tablespoon canola oil
3/4 pound venison tenderloin, cut into 1/2-inch-thick medallions
2 cups frozen broccoli pieces
1 medium red bell pepper, cut into thin 2-inch-long strips
1/2 cup snow peas
1/2 cup fresh mushrooms, sliced
1/4 cup water chestnuts, sliced
1/2 cup boiling water
2 teaspoons chicken-flavored instant bouillon granules, or 2 bouillon cubes
1/4 cup cold water
1 tablespoon cornstarch
1 teaspoon basil
1 teaspoon lime juice
1/2 cup sliced green onions

Heat the canola oil in a large skillet over medium heat. Add the venison medallions. Stir-fry until the venison is medium-rare. Do not overcook. Remove the venison to a serving plate. Add the broccoli, bell pepper, snow peas, mushrooms and water chestnuts. Stir-fry until the vegetables are tender-crisp. Combine the boiling water and bouillon granules in a small bowl. Stir to dissolve. Add the cold water, cornstarch, basil and lime juice. Stir well. Stir the cornstarch mixture into the vegetable mixture in the skillet. Cook, stirring, until the sauce thickens. Return the venison to the skillet to reheat. Sprinkle on green onions.

Makes 2 to 4 servings

Chicken Fettuccini with Champagne Sauce

4 boneless skinless chicken breasts
1 cup flour
Salt and white pepper to taste
2 to 3 tablespoons oil from oil-packed sun-dried tomatoes
1 1/2 cups Champagne or dry white wine
1 cup heavy cream
1/2 cup oil-packed julienne-cut sun-dried tomatoes
Cooked spinach fettuccini

Pound the chicken to an even thickness. Place the flour in a shallow bowl. Season with salt and white pepper and stir to mix. Dredge the chicken in the flour mixture.

Heat the tomato oil in a large skillet over medium-high heat. Add the chicken and brown on both sides. Add the Champagne and cook until the liquid is reduced by half and the chicken is cooked through. Remove the chicken and keep warm. Add the cream to the Champagne mixture and cook until the mixture starts to thicken. Add the sun-dried tomatoes and cook until heated through.

Arrange the spinach fettuccini on a serving plate. Top with the chicken. Pour the sauce over the chicken. Serve immediately. Recipe may be doubled.

Makes 4 servings

Penne with Gorgonzola and Pine Nuts

1 tablespoon oil from oil-packed sun-dried tomatoes
2 boneless skinless chicken breasts
1 pound penne
1 tablespoon oil from oil-packed sun-dried tomatoes
4 garlic cloves, minced
1/2 cup drained chopped oil-packed sun-dried tomatoes
1/2 cup chopped fresh basil
1/2 cup low-sodium chicken broth
1 cup (4 ounces) crumbled Gorgonzola cheese
1/4 cup chopped prosciutto
Salt and pepper to taste
1/4 cup pine nuts, toasted

Heat 1 tablespoon of the tomato oil in a large heavy skillet over medium-high heat.
Add the chicken and sauté 4 to 6 minutes per side, or until the chicken is cooked
through and the juices run clear. Remove the chicken and cool. Cut the chicken
into 1/2-inch pieces. Meanwhile, cook the pasta until al dente. Drain the pasta and
transfer to a large bowl.

Heat 1 tablespoon of the tomato oil in the same skillet over medium-high heat.
Add the garlic and sauté 1 minute, or until tender. Add the sun-dried tomatoes and
the chicken. Combine the basil, chicken broth, cheese and prosciutto in a bowl and
stir into the skillet. Bring the mixture to a boil. Add the chicken mixture to the
pasta and toss to coat. Season with salt and pepper. Top with the pine nuts.

Makes 4 servings

Pesto Shrimp

1 cup packed fresh basil
1/2 cup olive oil
1/4 cup fresh lemon juice
3 large garlic cloves, coarsely chopped
2 tablespoons grated Parmesan cheese
1 teaspoon grated lemon zest
3/4 teaspoon salt
1/2 teaspoon pepper
1 1/4 pounds large shrimp, peeled and deveined (40 shrimp)
12 ounces orzo or small bow tie pasta
2 tablespoons olive oil

Place the basil, 1/2 cup olive oil, lemon juice, garlic, cheese, lemon zest, salt and pepper in a food processor. Blend the ingredients until smooth. Reserve 1/4 cup of the marinade. Pour the remaining marinade into a resealable plastic bag. Add the shrimp. Refrigerate 30 to 40 minutes, tossing occasionally.

Cook the pasta and drain. Toss the pasta with 2 tablespoons olive oil in a bowl and keep warm. Arrange 5 shrimp on each of 8 bamboo skewers that have been soaked in warm water. Run a second skewer through the 5 shrimp to keep the shrimp from flipping during cooking. Grill the shrimp over medium-high heat about 3 minutes per side, or until the shrimp turn pink.

Spoon the pasta onto serving plates. Top each portion with 2 shrimp skewers. Heat the reserved marinade and drizzle it over the shrimp.

Makes 4 servings

Shrimp and Feta à la Grecque

1 pound medium shrimp, peeled, deveined and cooked
1 pound feta cheese, drained and coarsely crumbled
1 cup sliced scallions
1 cup tomato sauce
1/2 cup olive oil
1/4 cup lemon juice
1 tablespoon chopped fresh parsley
1 tablespoon chopped fresh basil
1 tablespoon chopped fresh dillweed
1/2 teaspoon salt
1/2 teaspoon pepper
1 1/2 pounds fettuccini or spinach fettuccini
Chopped tomatoes (optional)
Chopped black olives (optional)

Combine the shrimp, cheese and scallions in a large bowl. Add the tomato sauce, olive oil, lemon juice, parsley, basil, dillweed, salt and pepper. Mix well. Cover the bowl and refrigerate 1 hour.

Cook the pasta according to package directions. Drain. Toss the shrimp mixture with the hot pasta. Stir in the tomatoes and olives. Serve immediately, or refrigerate 1 hour and serve cold.

Makes 8 to 10 servings

Linguini with Clam Sauce

teaspoon salt

pound linguini

cup (1 stick) butter

garlic cloves, minced

cup minced onion

jars or cans minced clams, juice reserved

cup chopped fresh parsley

freshly grated Parmesan cheese

Fill a large stockpot with water and add the salt. Bring to a boil and add the linguini. Cook until the pasta is tender.

Melt the butter in a medium skillet. Add the garlic and onion and sauté until golden brown. Add the juice from the clams and simmer 5 minutes. Stir in the clams and parsley and simmer until heated through. Drain the linguini and place in a serving bowl. Pour the clam mixture over the linguini. Sprinkle with the cheese and serve immediately.

Makes 4 to 6 servings

Artichoke Linguini

Caper plants are small shrubs native to the Mediterranean area. Their buds are handpicked daily— the smaller the bud, the higher the quality.

1 pound linguini
2 tablespoons butter
2 tablespoons olive oil
1¹/2 tablespoons flour
1 cup chicken broth
1 garlic clove, minced
1 tablespoon minced fresh parsley
1 tablespoon lemon juice
¹/4 teaspoon pepper
¹/8 teaspoon salt
1 (14-ounce) can artichoke hearts, drained and quartered
3 tablespoons grated Parmesan cheese
2 teaspoons capers, drained
1 tablespoon butter
2 tablespoons olive oil
1 tablespoon grated Parmesan cheese

Cook the linguini according to package directions and keep warm. Heat 2 tablespoons butter and 2 tablespoons olive oil in a medium saucepan over low heat. Stir in the flour and cook, stirring, until the mixture is smooth and bubbles for 1 minute. Stir in the chicken broth and cook, stirring, 7 to 10 minutes, or until the mixture is thick. Add the garlic, parsley, lemon juice, pepper and salt. Cook for 3 to 5 minutes over low heat, stirring constantly. Add the artichoke hearts, 3 tablespoons cheese and the capers. Cover and simmer for 3 minutes.

Heat together 1 tablespoon butter, 2 tablespoons olive oil and 1 tablespoon cheese in a saucepan. Combine the butter mixture with the linguini and mix well. Add the artichoke sauce. Toss and serve immediately.

Makes 4 to 6 servings

Sun-Dried Tomato and Spinach Pasta

1 to 1^{1}/2 cups sun-dried tomatoes
^{2}/3 cup chicken broth
^{1}/3 cup extra-virgin olive oil
1 to 2 teaspoons minced garlic
^{1}/4 teaspoon salt
^{1}/2 teaspoon pepper
1 teaspoon oregano
1 teaspoon basil
6 ounces fresh spinach
6 tablespoons pine nuts, toasted
^{1}/2 cup (2 ounces) crumbled feta cheese
1 pound penne
2 tablespoons pine nuts, toasted
^{1}/4 cup (1 ounce) crumbled feta cheese

Place the tomatoes in a small bowl. Cover with hot water and set aside for
3 minutes to soften. Drain. Combine the chicken broth, olive oil, garlic, salt,
pepper, oregano and basil in a large skillet over medium-high heat. Add the
tomatoes and spinach and cook until the spinach wilts and is tender. Add
6 tablespoons pine nuts to the spinach. Add ^{1}/2 cup cheese to the spinach
mixture and melt in. Meanwhile, cook the penne in boiling water in a stockpot
according to package directions. Drain the penne and add to the spinach mixture.
Mix well. Sprinkle the penne with 2 tablespoons pine nuts and ^{1}/4 cup cheese.
Serve immediately.

Makes 4 servings

Herbed Ravioli with Pink Tomato Sauce

Pasta

2¹/4 cups flour
3 eggs, at room temperature
1 tablespoon olive oil
2 teaspoons milk

12 small Italian parsley leaves
12 small basil leaves
12 small sage leaves
¹/8 teaspoon salt, or to taste

Filling

²/3 cup ricotta cheese
¹/3 cup shredded whole milk or part-
    skim mozzarella cheese
¹/4 cup (1 ounce) grated Parmesan
    cheese

¹/8 teaspoon salt
¹/8 teaspoon freshly ground pepper
Several sprigs Italian parsley, basil and
    sage, chopped together

Pink Tomato Sauce

3 tablespoons butter
3 garlic cloves, minced
¹/4 teaspoon crushed red pepper flakes
¹/4 teaspoon salt

¹/2 cup tomato purée
1 cup heavy cream
1 tablespoon butter
¹/3 cup grated Parmesan cheese

Assembly

¹/4 cup chopped plum tomato
3 tablespoons (or more) julienne-cut sage leaves

For the pasta, place the flour in a food processor. Beat the eggs, olive oil and milk together in a bowl. Add most of the egg mixture to the flour and mix by pulsing until a rough dough forms. Add the remaining egg mixture if the dough is dry. Turn the dough out onto a board. Knead lightly using lightly floured hands for 10 minutes, or until the dough is satiny and smooth. Cover the dough with a towel and let rest for 15 minutes.

For the filling, combine the ricotta, mozzarella and Parmesan cheeses in a bowl. Stir in the salt, pepper and herbs. Refrigerate.

Cut the dough in half. Cut 1 half in half again to form 2 quarters. Working with 1 quarter, use a rolling pin to roll the dough as thinly as possible into a rough oblong, measuring about ¹/16-inch thick. If the dough sticks, dust it very lightly with flour.

Curl one side of the dough up onto the rolling pin and gently stretch the dough on the rolling pin. Stretch the dough from the center to the edges, while continuing to roll gently. Repeat with the other sides of the dough. Shape and roll the dough into a rough square, as thin as possible. Transfer the rolled dough onto a waxed paper-lined baking sheet. Repeat with the other dough quarter, making it as close to the shape of the first quarter as possible.

Brush one sheet of dough lightly with water, leaving a ¼-inch border at the edges. Choose herb leaves that are the same size. Rinse and pat dry. Arrange the herb leaves on the dough so that each leaf will eventually serve as the center of each ravioli square. Carefully place the second sheet of rolled dough over the first and roll both together until very thin, forming a rough 13-inch square. Trim the edges so the dough is a 12-inch square.

Roll out the remaining half of the dough to a 13-inch square and trim to 12 inches. Place rounded teaspoons of filling 1½ inches apart on the plain pasta to form 20 mounds of filling in a checkerboard pattern. With a wet finger, draw lines across and around the mounds and on the edges of the dough. Carefully lift the herb pasta sheet and place it over the filling. Run a finger around the mounds of fillings again, pressing down to seal the layers. With a fluted pastry wheel, cut out the ravioli. Cut a long strip first; then, 1 at a time, cut the strip into 2½- to 3-inch pieces around the fillings. Trim off any thick edges and press the edges together to seal. With a small spatula, place the ravioli on a lined baking sheet and cover with plastic wrap. Refrigerate up to 1 day.

For the sauce, melt 3 tablespoons butter in a heavy medium saucepan over medium heat. Add the garlic, red pepper flakes and salt. Cook and stir for 1½ minutes, or until the mixture is fragrant. Stir in the tomato purée and bring to a boil. Reduce the heat to very low and simmer 5 minutes to blend flavors, stirring occasionally. Gradually stir the cream into the sauce. Increase the heat slightly and bring just to a simmer, stirring constantly. Cut 1 tablespoon butter into small pieces and stir into the sauce. Remove the sauce from the heat and stir in the Parmesan cheese. Cover and keep warm.

Bring a large stockpot of water to a boil. Add ⅛ teaspoon salt. Gently add the ravioli and cook 11 to 13 minutes, stirring gently, or until the pasta is tender. Don't boil too vigorously. Drain carefully; transfer to heated pasta bowls. Spoon sauce over and around ravioli. Sprinkle each serving with chopped tomato and sage strips.

Makes 4 servings

Layered Pasta Ricotta Pie

1 pound spaghetti or vermicelli
1 tablespoon olive oil
1/3 cup finely chopped onion
4 garlic cloves, finely chopped
1/2 cup (2 ounces) grated Romano cheese
1 egg
2 egg yolks
1 pound ricotta cheese
1 (10-ounce) package frozen spinach, thawed and drained well
1/2 teaspoon salt
1/2 cup (2 ounces) grated Romano cheese
2 egg whites
1 (48-ounce) jar pasta sauce

Break the pasta into thirds. Cook in boiling water in a stockpot according to package directions until al dente. Drain.

Meanwhile, heat the olive oil in a large skillet. Add the onion and garlic and cook until tender. Remove from the heat. Add the cooked pasta, 1/2 cup Romano cheese and 1 egg. Mix well. Press the pasta into a well-greased 9-inch springform pan. Combine the egg yolks, ricotta cheese, spinach, salt and 1/2 cup Romano cheese in a bowl. Spread the spinach mixture over the pasta.

Beat the egg whites in a small bowl with an electric mixer until stiff. Gently fold in 1 1/2 cups pasta sauce. Spoon the egg white mixture over the spinach. Bake at 350 degrees for 50 to 60 minutes. Remove the pan from the oven and let stand 10 minutes. Remove the springform ring. Cut the pie into wedges and serve with the remaining pasta sauce.

Makes 8 servings

Pasta with Ricotta and Roasted Red Pepper Sauce

1 pound pasta, any shape
Roasted Red Pepper Sauce (below)

Cook the pasta in boiling water in a stockpot according to package directions. Drain well. Combine the pasta with the sauce in a bowl and toss to mix.

Makes 4 servings

Roasted Red Pepper Sauce

3 tablespoons olive oil
2 garlic cloves, minced
3 roasted red bell peppers, cored, seeded and diced
1/3 cup chopped fresh basil
1 cup ricotta cheese
7 tablespoons freshly grated Romano or Parmesan cheese
Salt and freshly ground pepper to taste

Heat the olive oil in a saucepan. Add the garlic and sauté 1 to 2 minutes. Add the bell peppers, basil, ricotta cheese and Romano cheese. Season with salt and pepper. Cook over low heat until very hot, but do not boil.

Makes about 2 1/2 cups

Penne with Vodka and Spicy Tomato Cream Sauce

1/4 cup olive oil
2 to 3 links hot sausage
4 garlic cloves, minced
1/2 teaspoon crushed red pepper flakes
1 (28-ounce) can crushed tomatoes
3/4 teaspoon salt
1 pound penne
2 tablespoons vodka
1 cup heavy cream
1/4 cup chopped fresh parsley

Heat the olive oil in a large skillet. Remove and discard the sausage casings. Place
the sausage in the skillet. Cook until browned, stirring until crumbly. Add the
garlic and red pepper flakes and cook, stirring, until the garlic is golden brown. Add
the tomatoes and salt and bring the mixture to a boil. Reduce the heat to low and
simmer 10 minutes. Cook the pasta in boiling water in a stockpot according to
package directions. Drain. Add the vodka and cream to the tomato sauce and bring
to a boil. Stir in the pasta and cook 1 minute. Add the parsley and serve.

Makes 4 servings

Polenta Lasagna

Polenta Lasagna

3 cups milk
1 tablespoon butter
1 teaspoon sugar
1/2 teaspoon salt
1 cup stone-ground yellow cornmeal
1/4 cup (1 ounce) freshly grated Parmesan cheese
2 to 3 links hot Italian sausage (optional)
5 tablespoons freshly grated Parmesan cheese
2 cups spaghetti sauce
5 tablespoons freshly grated Parmesan cheese
8 ounces fresh mozzarella cheese, sliced

Combine the milk, butter, sugar and salt in a large heavy saucepan. Heat to a simmer. Gradually add the cornmeal, whisking constantly. Reduce the heat and stir with a wooden spoon until the polenta pulls away from the side of the pan. Remove from the heat and stir in 1/4 cup Parmesan cheese.

Remove the sausage casings and break the sausage into small pieces. Brown in a medium skillet, stirring until crumbly. Spread the polenta in a buttered 9x13-inch casserole dish. Sprinkle with 5 tablespoons Parmesan cheese. Add the sausage and spoon on the spaghetti sauce. Sprinkle with 5 tablespoons Parmesan cheese and top with the sliced mozzarella cheese. Bake at 375 degrees for 30 minutes, or until bubbly. Place the dish under the broiler for 2 minutes to brown. Let the dish stand for 10 to 15 minutes before serving.

Makes 6 servings

Eggplant Parmesan

Choose eggplant that is firm, glossy, heavy, and free of brown spots. The flesh should spring back when lightly pressed. Eggplant can be stored in a perforated plastic bag in the refrigerator for several days.

1/4 cup extra-virgin olive oil
2 garlic cloves, minced
1 (28-ounce) can crushed Italian tomatoes
Salt and pepper to taste
1 cup flour
3 eggs
1 1/2 cups bread crumbs
1 large eggplant
3/4 cup extra-virgin olive oil
12 basil leaves, torn
1/4 cup (1 ounce) grated Parmigiano-Reggiano cheese
3/4 cup (3 ounces) shredded provolone cheese

Heat 1/4 cup olive oil in a medium saucepan. Add the garlic and sauté 1 minute. Add the tomatoes and season with salt and pepper. Simmer 30 minutes. Place the flour in a shallow dish. Beat the eggs in a second dish. Place the bread crumbs in a third dish and season with salt and pepper. Set aside.

Peel and trim the eggplant. Slice crosswise into 1/2-inch slices. Dredge each eggplant slice in flour, then eggs, then bread crumbs. Heat 3/4 cup olive oil in a large skillet over medium heat. Add the breaded eggplant slices and cook 2 to 3 minutes per side. Spread a thin layer of the tomato sauce in the bottom of a 9x12-inch baking dish. Arrange the eggplant over the sauce. Top with the remaining tomato sauce. Scatter the basil over the sauce and sprinkle with Parmigiano-Reggiano cheese. Cover with the provolone cheese. Bake at 375 degrees for 20 minutes.

Makes 4 servings

Barbecue Sauce

2 cups ketchup
1 cup packed brown sugar
3/4 cup apple cider vinegar

1/4 cup water
1 tablespoon Worcestershire sauce

Combine the ketchup, brown sugar, vinegar, water and Worcestershire sauce in a heavy saucepan. Simmer the mixture 25 minutes, stirring occasionally. Serve over chicken or ribs. This sauce can be refrigerated several days.

Makes about 4 cups

Bolognese Sauce

3 tablespoons butter
1 tablespoon olive oil
1/2 cup chopped yellow onion
2/3 cup chopped celery
2/3 cup chopped carrots
1/2 pound ground lean chuck
1/4 pound ground pork

Salt and pepper to taste
1 cup milk
1/8 teaspoon nutmeg
1 cup dry white wine
2 cups chopped canned Italian
   tomatoes

Heat the butter and olive oil in a Dutch oven. Add the onion and sauté until translucent. Add the chopped celery and carrots and sauté 2 minutes longer. Add the ground chuck and pork and season with salt and pepper. Cook the meat, but take care not to brown it. Add the milk and nutmeg and simmer until the milk evaporates. Add the wine and cook until the wine evaporates. Add the tomatoes and simmer on low for 3 hours. Serve over pasta.

Makes 8 servings

FINISHES

desserts

hot beverages

Carrot Cake

Cake
2 cups sugar
4 eggs
1 cup applesauce
1/2 cup vegetable oil
2 teaspoons baking soda
2 teaspoons cinnamon

1 teaspoon salt
2 cups flour
2 cups grated carrots
1 cup chopped walnuts
1 cup raisins

Cream Cheese Frosting
8 ounces cream cheese, softened
6 tablespoons vegetable shortening

2 teaspoons vanilla extract
4 cups confectioners' sugar

For the cake, beat the sugar, eggs, applesauce and vegetable oil in a large bowl until smooth. Mix the baking soda, cinnamon and salt together in a bowl. Add to the egg mixture. Stir in the flour. Stir in the carrots, walnuts and raisins with a heavy spoon. Pour the batter into a greased 9x13-inch cake pan. Bake at 325 degrees 1 hour. Cool completely.

For the frosting, beat the cream cheese and shortening together in a bowl with an electric mixer. Add the vanilla and confectioners' sugar and beat at high speed until the frosting is smooth and light. Spread over the cooled cake.

Makes 10 to 12 servings

Seven-Minute Frosting

2 egg whites
1 1/2 cups sugar
1 1/2 teaspoons light corn syrup

1/3 cup cold water
1/8 teaspoon salt, or to taste
1 teaspoon vanilla extract

Place the egg whites, sugar, corn syrup, cold water and salt in the top of a double boiler over simmering water. Mix the ingredients thoroughly. Cook, beating the egg white mixture constantly with a rotary or electric beater, 7 to 12 minutes, or until the mixture forms peaks. Remove from the heat. Add the vanilla and beat until the mixture is spreading consistency.

Makes enough frosting to cover a 3-layer cake

Pictured on overleaf: Lemon Cake (page 177)

Chocolate Cake

This recipe, from western Iowa, was passed along years ago during a party line telephone conversation. Party line calls were much like modern conference calls, except the party-liners were your neighbors. Each residence had a distinctive ring (for example, four short rings; one long and two short rings; and so on); if the telephone rang continuously, it was an emergency. You reached the operator with one ring.

1/2 cup (1 stick) butter, softened
1 1/2 cups sugar
2 eggs, lightly beaten
2 squares unsweetened chocolate, melted
1 teaspoon baking soda
2 cups cake flour, sifted once before measuring

1 cup cold brewed tea, preferably orange pekoe
1 teaspoon vanilla extract
Cocoa Frosting (optional, below)
Seven-Minute Frosting (optional, page 172)

Combine the butter and sugar in a bowl. Add the eggs and mix well with an electric mixer. Add the melted chocolate and beat until the batter is creamy. Sift the baking soda and flour together 3 times. Alternately add the flour mixture and the tea to the chocolate mixture. Add the vanilla. Pour the cake batter into a greased and floured 9x13-inch cake pan or 2 round layer pans. Bake at 350 degrees about 35 minutes, or until the cake tests done. Remove the cake from the oven and cool completely. Frost with Cocoa Frosting or Seven-Minute Frosting.

Makes 12 servings

Cocoa Frosting

1 cup sugar
1/4 cup (1/2 stick) butter, softened
1/4 cup baking cocoa

1/4 cup cream or milk
Milk

Place the sugar, butter, cocoa and cream in a medium saucepan over medium-high heat. Stir the mixture constantly while bringing to a boil. Let the chocolate mixture boil vigorously for 1 minute. Remove from the heat and cool several minutes. Beat the frosting until creamy, adding a few drops of milk to keep the frosting from becoming too hard.

Makes about 1 1/2 cups

Cranberry Almond Pound Cake

Cake

1/2 cup dried cranberries
1/4 cup amaretto or water
3 cups flour
1/2 teaspoon salt
1 1/4 teaspoons baking powder
1/2 teaspoon baking soda
4 ounces almond paste
1/2 teaspoon almond extract

2 1/2 cups sugar
1 cup (2 sticks) plus 2 tablespoons
    butter, softened
6 eggs
1 cup sour cream
2 cups fresh or thawed frozen
    cranberries

Amaretto Glaze

1 1/2 cups confectioners' sugar
2 tablespoons amaretto, or 1 1/2 tablespoons water

For the cake, place the dried cranberries and amaretto in a small saucepan and heat. Set aside to cool for 2 hours, stirring occasionally, until the fruit soaks up all the liquid.

Sift together the flour, salt, baking powder and baking soda in a bowl and set aside. Combine the almond paste, almond extract and sugar in a bowl. Beat with an electric mixer until the ingredients look like wet sand. Add the butter and beat 3 minutes, or until the mixture is fluffy. Add the eggs 1 at a time and beat until blended. Beat in 1/3 of the flour mixture and 1/3 of the sour cream. Repeat, adding the flour mixture and the sour cream twice more. Beat the batter for 20 seconds, or until smooth. Fold in the fresh cranberries and the amaretto-soaked cranberries. Pour the batter into a greased and floured bundt pan. Bake at 350 degrees for 50 to 60 minutes. Cool the cake in the pan for 20 minutes. Turn out onto a wire rack or plate.

For the glaze, sift the confectioners' sugar into a bowl. Gradually blend in the amaretto until the glaze is smooth. Drizzle the warm cake with the glaze.

Makes 16 servings

The cranberry is one of only three fruits that can trace their roots to North American soil. The other two are the Concord grape and the blueberry.

Chocolate and Chestnut Yule Log

7 tablespoons heavy cream
8 ounces good-quality semisweet
   chocolate (not chocolate chips),
   broken into pieces
1/2 cup (1 stick) unsalted butter,
   softened
8 eggs
1 1/4 cups sugar

1 1/3 cups flour
2/3 cup baking cocoa
1 teaspoon baking powder
1 ounce fructose
2 tablespoons water
1/4 cup rum
1/3 cup whipping cream
2/3 cup canned chestnut cream

Pour 7 tablespoons heavy cream into a saucepan and bring to a boil. Remove from the heat. Add the chocolate pieces and beat until the chocolate melts. Cool the mixture to lukewarm and beat in the butter. Let the mixture stand 4 hours, or until thick.

Combine the eggs and sugar in a double boiler set over low heat. Beat until lukewarm. Remove from the heat and beat for 10 minutes. Add the flour, cocoa and baking powder and blend in with a spatula.

Pour the batter onto a waxed paper-lined baking sheet. Bake at 375 degrees for 12 minutes. Cool for 5 minutes and remove from the baking sheet. Combine the fructose, water and rum and brush the cake layer with the mixture. Beat 1/3 cup whipping cream in a bowl with an electric mixer until stiff peaks form. Gently fold the whipped cream into the chestnut cream.

Spread the chestnut mixture over the cake layer and roll the cake layer from the far short end forward. Diagonally slice the ends off each side of the cake. Attach 1 or both ends to the top of the cake as knots in the log. Gently frost the cake with the chocolate mixture. Place the cake on a platter and decorate with holiday greens.

Makes 10 servings

Gingerbread Cake

¹/2 cup (1 stick) butter, softened
1 cup sugar
1 teaspoon baking soda
1 cup hot water
2¹/2 cups sifted flour
¹/8 teaspoon salt
1 teaspoon ginger
1 teaspoon cinnamon
1 cup light molasses, or slightly less dark molasses
Whipped cream

Cream the butter and sugar together in a large bowl with an electric mixer until light and fluffy. Combine the baking soda and hot water in a small bowl and stir to dissolve the baking soda. Add the baking soda mixture to the butter mixture and blend. Add the flour, salt, ginger and cinnamon and mix well. Add the molasses and mix well.

Pour the batter into a 9-inch-square pan and bake at 325 degrees for 25 to 35 minutes. Serve with whipped cream.

Makes 9 servings

In the nineteenth century, English pubs kept shakers of ginger on their counters so the patrons could shake the spice into their drinks. This was the origin of ginger ale.

Lemon Cake

Cake

3 cups flour
3/4 teaspoon baking soda
1 teaspoon baking powder
3/4 teaspoon salt
4 egg whites
1/8 teaspoon salt, or to taste

1 cup (2 sticks) butter, softened
1 1/4 cups sugar
4 egg yolks
1 tablespoon finely grated lemon zest
1/4 cup lemon juice
1 cup milk

Lemon Syrup

1/3 cup sugar
2 tablespoons lemon juice
2 tablespoons hot water

For the cake, combine the flour, baking soda, baking powder and 3/4 teaspoon salt in a bowl and set aside. Beat the egg whites with 1/8 teaspoon salt in a bowl with an electric mixer until soft peaks form. Set aside. Cream the butter and sugar in a large bowl with a mixer until light abd fluffy. Add the egg yolks to the butter mixture 1 at a time, beating well. Add the lemon zest. Combine the lemon juice and milk in a small bowl. Add the flour mixture to the creamed butter, alternating with the lemon juice mixture. Fold in the egg whites. Spread the batter evenly in a greased 9-inch springform pan. Bake at 350 degrees for 55 to 65 minutes. Remove from the oven.

For the syrup, combine the sugar, lemon juice and hot water in a small bowl. Stir until the sugar dissolves. Spoon the syrup on top of the warm cake and let it stand. The syrup will crystallize as the cake cools.

Makes 12 to 16 servings

Almond Crescents

1 cup (2 sticks) butter, softened
1/3 cup sugar
2/3 cup ground blanched almonds
1²/3 cups sifted flour

1/4 teaspoon salt
1 cup confectioners' sugar
1 teaspoon cinnamon

Beat together the butter, sugar and blanched almonds in a bowl with an electric mixer until thoroughly mixed. Sift the flour and salt together in a bowl and gradually blend into the butter mixture. Chill the dough.

Roll out portions of the dough into pencil-thick strips. Cut into 2¹/2-inch lengths. Form into crescents on a cookie sheet. Bake at 325 degrees 14 to 16 minutes, or until the cookies are set but not brown. Cool the cookies until slightly warm. Combine the confectioners' sugar and cinnamon in a bowl. Carefully dip the cookies in the confectioners' sugar mixture.

Makes about 1¹/2 dozen

W. K. Kellogg and C. W. Post invented and sold cold breakfast cereals, turning the small town of Battle Creek, Michigan, into the "Cereal Bowl of the World" in the early part of the twentieth century.

Pecan Crispies

1 cup (2 sticks) butter, softened
1 cup sugar
1 cup packed brown sugar
1 egg
1 teaspoon vanilla extract
1 teaspoon baking soda
1 teaspoon cream of tartar

1 teaspoon salt
3¹/2 cups flour
1 cup vegetable oil
1 cup crispy rice cereal
1 cup pecans, chopped
1 cup rolled oats

Cream the butter, sugar and brown sugar in a large bowl with an electric mixer until light and fluffy. Add the egg and vanilla. Combine the baking soda, cream of tartar, salt and flour in a bowl. Alternately beat the vegetable oil and the flour mixture into the creamed butter and sugar. Fold in the cereal, pecans and oats. Drop the batter by the tablespoon onto a greased cookie sheet. Bake the cookies at 350 degrees for 10 to 12 minutes. Cool on a wire rack.

Makes about 4 dozen

Caramel Bars

1 (14-ounce) package caramel candies
1/3 cup milk
2 cups flour
2 cups quick-cooking or regular oats
1 1/2 cups packed light brown sugar
1 teaspoon baking soda
1/2 teaspoon salt
1 egg
1 cup (2 sticks) butter, softened
1 cup (6 ounces) semisweet chocolate chips
1 cup chopped walnuts

Combine the candies and milk in a 2-quart saucepan and heat over low heat, stirring frequently until smooth. Set aside.

Mix the flour, oats, brown sugar, baking soda, salt and egg together in a bowl. Stir in the butter with a fork until the mixture is crumbly. Press half the flour mixture into a greased 9x13-inch baking pan. Bake at 350 degrees for 10 minutes. Remove the pan from the oven. Sprinkle the crust with the chocolate chips and walnuts. Drizzle with the caramel mixture. Sprinkle the remaining flour mixture on top. Bake at 350 degrees 25 minutes, or until the topping is golden brown. Cool for 30 minutes; then loosen the edges of the pan. Cool completely and cut into bars.

Makes 15 servings

Michigan Jumbles

1 1/4 cups flour
3/4 teaspoon baking soda
1/2 teaspoon cinnamon
1/8 teaspoon salt
3/4 cup chopped walnuts
3/4 cup chopped almonds
3/4 cup chopped pecans
1/2 cup dried cherries
1 cup dried cranberries
1 cup semisweet chocolate chips
1/2 cup (1 stick) unsalted butter, softened
3/4 cup sugar
1/4 cup packed brown sugar
1 egg
1 teaspoon vanilla extract

Sift the flour, baking soda, cinnamon and salt together into a large bowl. Add
the walnuts, almonds, pecans, cherries, cranberries and chocolate chips. Set aside.
Cream the butter, sugar and brown sugar in a bowl with an electric mixer until
light and fluffy. Add the egg and vanilla. Beat in the flour-nut mixture. Drop the
batter by spoonfuls onto a greased cookie sheet. Bake at 375 degrees for 12 to
15 minutes.

Makes 3 to 4 dozen

Cherry Pineapple Bars

Crust
2 cups flour
1 cup packed brown sugar
1/2 teaspoon salt
1 cup (2 sticks) butter

Topping
1/2 cup sugar
2 tablespoons cornstarch
1 (8-ounce) can crushed pineapple
2 egg yolks, beaten
1 cup maraschino cherries, chopped

For the crust, combine the flour, brown sugar and salt in a bowl. Cut in the butter until the mixture is crumbly. Set aside 1 cup of the crumb mixture. Press the remaining crumb mixture into a 9x13-inch baking pan. Bake at 350 degrees for 15 minutes. Remove from the oven and cool slightly while making the topping.

For the topping, combine the sugar, cornstarch, undrained pineapple and egg yolks in a saucepan. Cook over medium heat, stirring constantly, until the mixture thickens and bubbles. Remove from the heat and stir in the cherries. Spread the pineapple mixture evenly over the crust. Sprinkle on the reserved crumb mixture. Bake at 350 degrees for 30 minutes. Cool before cutting into bars.

Makes 2 1/2 dozen

Cream Wafers

Wafers
1 cup (2 sticks) butter
1/3 cup cream
2 cups flour
Sugar

Creamy Butter Frosting
1/4 cup (1/2 stick) butter, softened
3/4 cup confectioners' sugar
1 teaspoon vanilla extract
Milk (optional)

Assembly
Coarse colored sugar

For the wafers, mix the butter, cream and flour thoroughly in a bowl with an electric mixer. Chill 1 hour in the refrigerator. Take out a small portion of dough, keeping the rest refrigerated. Roll dough 1/8-inch thick on a floured board. Cut the dough into 1 1/2-inch rounds. Sprinkle the sugar on a sheet of waxed paper. Dip the cookies on both sides in the sugar to coat heavily. Place the cookies on a cookie sheet. Pierce the cookies in 4 places using a fork. Bake at 375 degrees for 7 to 10 minutes. Remove the cookies and cool.

For the frosting, blend the butter, confectioners' sugar and vanilla in a bowl with an electric mixer. Add a few drops of milk if the frosting is too thick to spread.

To assemble, spread the frosting on top of each cookie, then dip the cookies into the colored sugar.

Makes 5 to 7 dozen

Lemon Love Notes

Crust
1/2 cup (1 stick) butter, softened
1 cup flour
1/4 cup confectioners' sugar

Filling
2 to 3 tablespoons lemon juice
Grated zest of 1 lemon
2 eggs, beaten
1 cup sugar
2 tablespoons flour
1/2 teaspoon baking powder

Frosting
3/4 cup confectioners' sugar
2 tablespoons (about) orange juice

For the crust, blend the butter, flour and confectioners' sugar in a medium bowl with an electric mixer. Press into a 9-inch-square baking pan and bake at 350 degrees 15 minutes. Remove from the oven.

For the filling, place the lemon juice, lemon zest, eggs, sugar, flour and baking powder in a bowl. Mix with an electric mixer until smooth. Pour the lemon filling over the crust. Bake at 350 degrees 25 minutes, or until the filling is set. Remove from the oven and cool to room temperature.

For the frosting, stir together the confectioners' sugar and 2 tablespoons orange juice, or enough orange juice to make a smooth mixture. Gently spread over the filling. Cut into bars to serve.

Makes 12 to 16 servings

Orange Cookies

Cookies
1 cup vegetable shortening
2 cups sugar
2 eggs, beaten
Juice of 1 orange
Grated zest of 1 orange
4 1/2 cups flour
2 teaspoons baking powder
1 teaspoon baking soda
1 cup milk

Orange Frosting
2 tablespoons butter, softened
1 cup confectioners' sugar
Juice of 1 orange
Grated zest of 1 orange

For the cookies, cream together the shortening and sugar in a large bowl with an electric mixer until light and fluffy. Add the eggs to the shortening mixture. Beat in the orange juice and orange zest. Sift together the flour, baking powder and baking soda. Alternately add the flour mixture and milk to the shortening, mixing well. Drop the dough by teaspoons onto a greased and floured cookie sheet. Bake at 350 degrees for 8 to 10 minutes, or until lightly browned. Cool.

For the frosting, blend the butter, confectioners' sugar, orange juice and orange zest in a bowl with a mixer. Spread on the cooled cookies.

Makes 4 to 5 dozen

Brown Sugar Pecan Cookies

Cookies

1 cup (2 sticks) butter, softened
1/2 cup sugar
1/2 cup packed brown sugar
1 egg
1 teaspoon vanilla extract

2 cups flour
1/2 teaspoon baking soda
1/4 teaspoon salt
1/2 cup finely chopped pecans

Brown Sugar Frosting

1 cup packed brown sugar
1/2 cup half-and-half
1 tablespoon butter

1 1/2 to 1 2/3 cups sifted confectioners'
  sugar

Assembly

Pecan halves (optional)

For the cookies, beat the butter in a bowl with an electric mixer at medium speed until creamy. Gradually add the sugar and brown sugar, mixing well. Add the egg and vanilla. Beat well.

Combine the flour, baking soda and salt in a bowl. Gradually add to the butter mixture, mixing after each addition. Stir in the chopped pecans. Cover the dough and refrigerate for 30 minutes.

Shape the dough into 1-inch balls and place on cookie sheets. Bake at 350 degrees for 10 to 12 minutes. Cool the cookies on a wire rack.

For the frosting, combine the brown sugar and half-and-half in a saucepan. Cook over medium heat, stirring, until the mixture comes to a boil. Boil for 4 minutes. Remove from the heat and stir in the butter. Add 1 1/2 cups confectioners' sugar and beat with a mixer at medium speed until the frosting is smooth. Gradually add enough of the remaining confectioners' sugar to make a spreading consistency.

To assemble, spread the frosting on the cookies. Top each cookie with a pecan half.

Makes 5 dozen

Pumpkin Cookies with Caramel Frosting

Cookies
1 cup vegetable shortening
1 cup sugar
1 cup pumpkin
2 cups flour
1 tablespoon cinnamon
1/2 teaspoon salt
1 teaspoon baking soda

Caramel Frosting
4 1/2 tablespoons butter
2 tablespoons milk
3/4 cup packed brown sugar
2 cups (or more) confectioners' sugar
1 teaspoon vanilla extract

For the cookies, mix the shortening, sugar and pumpkin together in a bowl with
an electric mixer. Mix together the flour, cinnamon, salt and baking soda in a bowl.
Mix the flour mixture into the pumpkin mixture. Drop the dough by spoonfuls
onto cookie sheets. Bake at 350 degrees for 10 to 12 minutes. Prepare the frosting
while the cookies are baking.

For the frosting, melt the butter in a medium saucepan. Add the milk and brown
sugar and mix until the brown sugar is dissolved. Add the confectioners' sugar and
vanilla. Mix until the frosting is thick and creamy. Add more confectioners' sugar
to make a spreading consistency, if necessary. Spread the frosting on the hot
cookies. Cool before serving.

Makes 3 dozen

Heavenly Sugar Cookies

4 cups flour
1 teaspoon salt
1 teaspoon baking soda
1 teaspoon cream of tartar
1 cup sugar
1 cup confectioners' sugar
1 cup (2 sticks) butter, softened
1 cup vegetable oil
2 eggs
1 1/2 teaspoons vanilla extract
Sugar

Sift the flour into a bowl and add the salt, baking soda and cream of tartar. Set aside. Combine the sugar, confectioners' sugar, butter, vegetable oil, eggs and vanilla in a large bowl and beat well with an electric mixer. Sift the flour mixture again and gradually combine with the sugar mixture. Refrigerate the dough for 1 hour. Roll the dough into balls the diameter of a quarter. Place the dough on a lightly greased cookie sheet. Press the bottom of a glass into sugar; then press the glass into a cookie, making it almost flat. Bake at 350 degrees for 10 to 15 minutes.

Makes 4 dozen

Rugalach

16 ounces cream cheese, softened
2 cups (4 sticks) butter, softened
4 cups flour
Sugar
1 3/4 cups sugar
2 heaping tablespoons cinnamon
8 ounces walnuts, finely chopped

Beat the cream cheese and butter together in a large bowl with an electric mixer. Beat in the flour a little at a time. Knead until all the flour has been added. Refrigerate the dough overnight. Remove the dough and let it come to room temperature. Divide the dough into portions about the size of pie crust dough. Roll out 1 piece at a time on a well-floured surface to a 10- to 11-inch circle. Sprinkle the dough with 1 teaspoon sugar.

Mix together 1 3/4 cups sugar, the cinnamon and walnuts in a bowl. Sprinkle a light even layer over the dough. Cut the circle into wedges like a pizza. Roll each wedge from the wide end to the point. Repeat with all the slices. Repeat with the rest of the dough and sugar mixture. Dip the cookies in additional sugar. Place the cookies on a greased cookie sheet. Bake at 350 degrees for 20 to 30 minutes, checking to make sure the cookies don't burn. Remove the cookies and cool on a wire rack.

Makes 65 cookies

Probably the most popular of the American Jewish cookies, this horn-shaped treat was made with butter in Europe. The recipe was brought to this country by Eastern European Jewish immigrants. Cream cheese was added to the recipe later.

Glazed Apple Pie

Crust

2 egg yolks, beaten
Milk
2¹/2 cups flour
1 tablespoon sugar

1 teaspoon salt
1 cup (2 sticks) butter, softened
1 teaspoon grated lemon zest

Filling

2 cups cornflakes, crushed
10 apples, peeled and sliced
1 cup sugar
1 teaspoon cinnamon

¹/8 teaspoon nutmeg, or to taste
1 teaspoon lemon juice
Butter
2 egg whites

Lemon Glaze

1 cup confectioners' sugar
1 teaspoon lemon juice
2 to 3 tablespoons milk

For the crust, place the egg yolks in a 1-cup measuring cup. Add enough milk to measure ²/3 cup. Pour into a bowl. Add the flour, sugar, salt, butter and lemon zest and work into a dough. Divide the dough into 2 portions, with 1 portion slightly larger than the other. Refrigerate the dough until firm. Roll out the larger ball of dough to fit a greased jelly roll pan.

For the filling, place the cornflakes on the dough. Combine the apples, sugar, cinnamon, nutmeg and lemon juice in a bowl. Place the apple filling on the cornflakes and dot with butter. Roll out the second piece of dough to the size of the pan and place on top of the apples. Make vent holes in the top crust. Beat the egg whites and brush over the top crust. Bake at 350 degrees for 45 minutes.

For the glaze, combine the confectioners' sugar, lemon juice and milk in a bowl and beat well. Drizzle the glaze over the pie while it is still hot. Serve with cream.

Makes 12 to 15 servings

Apple Rhubarb Pie

Filling

1/2 cup sugar
3/4 cup packed brown sugar
1 teaspoon cinnamon
4 large apples, peeled and sliced
2 cups chopped rhubarb
2 tablespoons sifted flour
1 unbaked pie pastry, prepared from Basic Pie Crust recipe (page 192), chilled

Topping

1/2 cup (1 stick) butter, softened
1/2 cup packed brown sugar
1 cup flour, sifted

For the filling, combine the sugar, brown sugar, cinnamon, apples, rhubarb and flour in a bowl. Mound the filling in a pastry-lined pie plate.

For the topping, cream together the butter and brown sugar in a bowl with an electric mixer. Cut in the flour to make a crumb topping mixture. Sprinkle the topping over the filling. Bake at 450 degrees for 10 minutes. Reduce the temperature to 350 degrees and bake for 45 minutes, or until done. If the pie browns too quickly, loosely cover with aluminum foil and continue baking. Serve with vanilla ice cream or whipped cream.

Makes 6 to 8 servings

Chocolate Pecan Pie

1 unbaked pie pastry, prepared from Basic Pie Crust recipe (page 192)
2 tablespoons flour
2 tablespoons sugar
3 eggs, lightly beaten
1/2 cup dark corn syrup
1 1/2 cups packed brown sugar
1 teaspoon vanilla extract
2 cups chopped pecans
2 to 4 ounces chocolate chips
Ice cream or whipped cream

Line a pie plate with the pastry. Combine the flour and sugar in a small bowl. Combine the flour mixture with the beaten eggs in a medium bowl and mix well. Add the corn syrup, brown sugar, vanilla, pecans and chocolate chips. Stir well. Pour the mixture into the pastry-lined pie plate. Bake at 425 degrees for 10 minutes. Reduce the temperature to 325 degrees and bake for 45 minutes. Serve with ice cream or whipped cream.

Makes 6 to 8 servings

Cherry Orchard Pie

1¹/4 cups sugar
2¹/2 tablespoons flour
¹/4 teaspoon salt
1 quart tart fresh red cherries, rinsed and pitted, or 2 cans frozen cherries, thawed
1 unbaked double-crust pie pastry, prepared from Basic Pie Crust recipe (below)

Mix the sugar, flour, salt and cherries together in a bowl. Fit 1 pie pastry into a pie plate. Spoon the cherry mixture into the pie plate. Top with the remaining pastry, sealing the edge and cutting vents. Bake at 450 degrees for 10 minutes. Reduce the temperature to 350 degrees and bake 25 minutes longer. If using frozen cherries reduce the sugar to 1 cup.

Makes 6 to 8 servings

The biggest cherry pie ever made was baked in a Traverse City, Michigan, bakery. The pie weighed over 14 tons and was over 17 feet wide.

Basic Pie Crust

2 cups flour
1 teaspoon salt
¹/2 teaspoon sugar (if making a dessert pie)
²/3 cup plus 1 tablespoon vegetable shortening
7 tablespoons (about) cold water

Mix the flour, salt and sugar together in a bowl. Cut the shortening into the flour with a fork until well mixed and granular. Add the cold water, using a little more or less to form a dough that sticks together. Continue to mix the dough by hand until it forms a ball. Do not overwork the dough. Divide the dough in half. Flatten into 2 disks. Wrap each in waxed paper and chill in the freezer 30 minutes. When ready to use, roll into a circle on a floured surface.

Makes enough for a double-crust pie

Orange Pie

Crust

1/2 cup (1 stick) butter, softened
3 tablespoons sugar

1 1/3 cups flour
1/4 teaspoon salt

Filling

1/4 cup orange juice
1 envelope unflavored gelatin
3 egg whites (see Note)
1/2 cup sugar
1/4 teaspoon cream of tartar
1/4 cup orange juice

3 egg yolks
1/2 cup sugar
1 teaspoon vanilla extract
1/4 teaspoon salt
8 ounces cream cheese, softened
1 cup whipping cream

For the crust, mix together the butter, sugar, flour and salt in a large bowl to form crumbs. Reserve 1/3 cup of the crumbs for the pie topping. Press the remaining crumbs into a 10-inch pie plate sprayed with nonstick cooking spray. Bake at 375 degrees for 10 minutes. Cool and set aside.

For the filling, pour 1/4 cup orange juice into the top of a double boiler over simmering water. Add the gelatin and stir to dissolve.

Beat the egg whites, 1/2 cup sugar and cream of tartar in a large bowl with an electric mixer until the egg whites are stiff; set aside. Combine 1/4 cup orange juice, the egg yolks, 1/2 cup sugar, vanilla and salt in a small saucepan. Beat with a mixer until the egg yolks are light. Add the egg yolk mixture to the gelatin. Cook, stirring constantly, over medium heat until the mixture thickens. Remove from the heat. Add the cream cheese and beat until smooth. Fold in the egg whites. Chill the mixture 30 minutes. Whip the cream and fold into the filling. Gently spoon the filling into the baked crust. Sprinkle on the reserved 1/3 cup crumbs. Chill.

Note: To avoid raw eggs that may carry salmonella, we suggest using an equivalent amount of powdered egg whites.

Makes 8 servings

SEASONS in THYME 193

Peach Melba Pie

Crust
1/4 cup caramel ice cream topping
2 tablespoons unsalted butter
4 cups broken vanilla wafers (about 30 wafers)

Filling
3 pints vanilla ice cream, softened
3/4 cup peach preserves
1/2 cup raspberry pourable fruit

Topping
1 cup raspberries
2 medium peaches, sliced
1/4 cup raspberry pourable fruit

For the crust, heat the caramel topping and butter in a small saucepan over low heat until the butter melts. Process the vanilla wafers in a food processor to form fine crumbs. Add the warm caramel mixture and process until the crumbs are moistened. Spoon the crumbs into a lightly greased 9-inch pie plate, pressing the crumbs onto the bottom and up the side. Set aside.

For the filling, put the ice cream in a large bowl. Add the peach preserves and stir until blended. Spread half the ice cream mixture onto the crust. Place the pie and the bowl in the freezer for 2 hours, or until the ice cream is firm. Remove the pie from the freezer and spread with the pourable fruit. Cover with the remaining peach-ice cream mixture. Freeze 4 hours, or until the filling is firm, or wrap the pie, airtight, and freeze up to 2 weeks. Remove the pie from the freezer 30 minutes before serving.

For the topping, combine the raspberries, peaches and pourable fruit in a bowl and mix well. Spoon over the pie filling. Refrigerate until serving time.

Makes 12 servings

Praline Pumpkin Pie

Filling
1 1/2 cups canned pumpkin
2 eggs, beaten
2 tablespoons flour
1/2 teaspoon salt
2 tablespoons molasses
1/2 cup sugar
2/3 cup packed brown sugar
3/4 teaspoon cinnamon
1 teaspoon pumpkin pie spice
1 1/2 cups evaporated milk
1 unbaked pie pastry, prepared from Basic Pie Crust recipe (page 192)

Topping
1/4 cup packed brown sugar
1 tablespoon butter
1/2 cup pecans, chopped

For the filling, beat the pumpkin, eggs, flour, salt, molasses, sugar, brown sugar, cinnamon and pumpkin pie spice in a large bowl with an electric mixer. Add the milk and mix well. Carefully pour the pumpkin mixture into a pastry-lined pie plate. Bake at 450 degrees for 10 minutes. Reduce the temperature to 325 degrees and continue to bake for 1 hour and 20 minutes.

For the topping, mix together the brown sugar, butter and pecans in a bowl. Sprinkle the topping over the pie and bake 10 minutes longer, or until the topping is golden brown.

Note: Although you may be tempted to use the last little bit of pumpkin in the can, don't do it. Measurements are the key to making this pie turn out perfectly.

Makes 6 to 8 servings

Chocolate Hazelnut Torte

Chocolate Crumb Crust
8 ounces chocolate wafer cookies, crushed
6 tablespoons unsalted butter, melted

Filling
8 ounces bittersweet chocolate, chopped
1 cup (2 sticks) unsalted butter, softened
1/2 teaspoon vanilla extract
6 tablespoons sugar
3 egg yolks (see Note)
1 cup baking cocoa
1 cup coarsely chopped blanched hazelnuts
1/8 teaspoon salt, or to taste
3 egg whites
2 tablespoons sugar
1/2 cup whipping cream, whipped
Hazelnut Caramel Sauce (page 197)

Assembly
Whipped cream
Hazelnuts

For the crust, mix the chocolate crumbs and melted butter with a fork in a bowl. Butter the bottom of a 9-inch springform pan. Pat the crumbs onto the side and bottom of the pan. Bake at 375 degrees 7 to 8 minutes, or until crisp. Cool the crust completely on a wire rack.

For the filling, melt the chocolate in the top of a double boiler set over hot, but not boiling, water. Set aside to cool. Cream the butter in a bowl with an electric mixer until very light and fluffy. Add the vanilla and beat until well blended. Beat in 6 tablespoons sugar until well blended. Beat in the egg yolks 1 at a time. Beat 4 to 5 minutes, or until the mixture is creamy. Beat in the cocoa 1/4 cup at a time until well blended. Add the cooled chocolate to the egg yolk mixture and beat just until blended. Fold in the hazelnuts.

Add the salt to the egg whites in a small bowl. Beat the egg whites with a mixer until they barely hold soft peaks. Beat in 2 tablespoons sugar and continue beating until the egg whites hold their shape when the beaters are raised. Gently fold the egg whites into the chocolate mixture. Fold in the whipped cream. Spoon the chocolate mixture into the prepared pan. Smooth the top. Cover with plastic wrap and refrigerate at least 5 hours.

Bring the hazelnut torte to room temperature about 20 minutes before serving. Remove the side of the springform pan. Set each torte slice on a pool of Hazelnut Caramel Sauce and garnish with whipped cream and hazelnuts.

Note: To avoid raw eggs that may carry salmonella, we suggest using an equivalent amount of pasteurized egg substitute and powdered egg whites.

Makes 10 servings

Hazelnut Caramel Sauce

1 1/2 cups cream
2/3 cup sugar
2 tablespoons water
1 tablespoon butter
1 tablespoon hazelnut liqueur, or to taste

Heat the cream in a small saucepan until hot. Place the sugar in a heavy-bottomed medium saucepan over medium heat. Using a wooden spoon, cook and stir constantly until the sugar melts and turns a light caramel color. Add the water and continue stirring until the sugar melts again. Gradually stir in the hot cream. Cook and stir until the mixture is smooth. Stir in the butter and cook, stirring, until the mixture thickens slightly. Remove from the heat and stir in the liqueur. Adjust the liqueur to taste. Cool completely, stirring occasionally. Serve at room temperature.

Makes about 2 1/2 cups

Lemon Ice

Juice of 1 1/2 lemons
Juice of 1 orange
1 cup sugar

1 teaspoon vanilla extract
1 cup whipping cream
1 cup milk

Pour the lemon juice and orange juice into a bowl. Stir in the sugar and vanilla and let stand a few minutes. Whip the cream in a large bowl with an electric mixer until stiff. Add the milk to the juice mixture. Blend the juice mixture into the whipped cream by hand or using a mixer at low speed. Pour the cream mixture into a 9-inch-square metal pan. Do not use a glass pan or the mixture won't freeze properly. Freeze until half solid. Remove the lemon ice from the freezer and stir by hand. Return to the freezer until firm.

Makes 10 to 12 servings

Frozen Strawberry Chantilly

Crust
1/2 cup (1 stick) butter, melted
1 cup flour

1/2 cup packed brown sugar

Filling
10 ounces fresh strawberries, sliced, or
   thawed frozen strawberries, sliced
1 egg white, beaten (see Note)
1 teaspoon vanilla extract

1 cup sugar
1 tablespoon lemon juice
1 pint whipping cream, whipped

For the crust, mix the butter, flour and brown sugar in a bowl. Reserve 1/4 of the mixture for topping. Pat the remainder into a 9x13-inch glass baking dish. Bake at 400 degrees for 15 minutes, stirring occasionally, or until golden brown. Cool.

For the filling, combine the strawberries, egg white, vanilla, sugar and lemon juice in a large bowl. Beat with an electric mixer for 15 to 20 minutes. Fold the whipped cream into the strawberry mixture. Gently spoon the mixture over the baked crumbs. Freeze until the filling is firm. Sprinkle on the reserved crumbs and serve.

Note: To avoid raw eggs that may carry salmonella, we suggest using an equivalent amount of powdered egg whites.

Makes 15 servings

Bavarian Apple Cheesecake

Crust and Bottom Layer

1/3 cup sugar
1/3 cup butter, softened
1 tablespoon vegetable shortening
1/4 teaspoon vanilla extract

1 cup flour
1/8 teaspoon salt
2 cups peeled cored sliced baking
   apples

Filling

16 ounces cream cheese, softened
1/2 cup sugar
1/2 teaspoon vanilla extract

2 eggs
2 cups peeled cored sliced baking
   apples

Topping

1/2 cup sugar
1/2 teaspoon vanilla extract

1 1/4 teaspoons cinnamon
1/4 to 1/2 cup sliced almonds

For the crust and bottom layer, combine the sugar, butter, shortening and vanilla in a medium bowl. Beat at medium speed with an electric mixer until well mixed. Mix in the flour and salt until the mixture is crumbly. Press the mixture onto the bottom of a 9-inch springform pan. Arrange the apple slices in a single layer on the crust. Cover with foil and bake at 400 degrees for 15 minutes. Remove from the oven and cool.

For the filling, beat the cream cheese, sugar and vanilla in a large bowl with an electric mixer until fluffy. Add the eggs all at once, beating at low speed just until mixed. Pour the cream cheese batter into the pan. Arrange the apple slices over the cream cheese.

For the topping, stir together the sugar, vanilla and cinnamon in a bowl. Sprinkle the sugar mixture and almonds on top of the filling. Bake at 400 degrees for 40 minutes, or until golden brown. Let cool. Remove the side of the pan and place the cheesecake on a platter. Cover and chill 6 to 24 hours before serving.

Makes 8 to 10 servings

Marzipan Cheesecake with Raspberry Sauce

1¹/2 cups finely crushed chocolate sandwich cookies (about 20 cookies)
1/4 cup (1/2 stick) butter, melted
24 ounces cream cheese, softened
1 (8-ounce) package almond paste, crumbled
1 cup sugar
4 eggs
1 cup sour cream
Raspberry Sauce (below)
Fresh raspberries

Combine the cookie crumbs and melted butter in a small bowl. Press onto the bottom of a greased 9-inch springform pan. Beat the cream cheese and almond paste in a large bowl on medium-high speed of an electric mixer until combined. Beat in the sugar until the mixture is fluffy. Add the eggs and sour cream all at once, beating on low speed just until combined. Pour the batter into the crust. Bake at 325 degrees for 1 hour, or until the center is almost set. Cool for 15 minutes. Loosen the crust from the side of the pan. Cool 30 minutes longer; remove the side of the pan. Cool completely. Chill the cheesecake for 4 to 6 hours. Serve the cheesecake with Raspberry Sauce and fresh raspberries.

Makes 12 servings

Raspberry Sauce

1 (12-ounce) package frozen unsweetened raspberries, thawed
1/2 cup sugar
1 teaspoon lemon juice

Place the raspberries in a blender container and blend until smooth. Press the berries through a sieve to remove the seeds. Combine the raspberry purée, sugar and lemon juice in a small saucepan. Heat, stirring, just until the sugar dissolves. Cool. Pour the sauce into a small container; cover and chill.

Makes about 1¹/2 cups

Chocolate Mousse with Grand Marnier

4 ounces sweet baking chocolate, broken into pieces
4 ounces semisweet chocolate, broken into pieces
1/4 cup Grand Marnier or other orange-flavored liqueur
2 cups whipping cream
1/2 cup sifted confectioners' sugar
Strips of orange zest (optional)
Whipped cream (optional)

Combine the sweet baking chocolate, semisweet chocolate and Grand Marnier
in top of a double boiler. Bring the water to a boil. Reduce the heat to low and
simmer until the chocolate melts. Cool the chocolate to lukewarm. The mixture
will thicken and look grainy.

Beat the whipping cream in a bowl with an electric mixer. Gradually add the
confectioners' sugar, beating until soft peaks form. Gently fold 1/4 of the whipped
cream mixture into the chocolate mixture; then fold in the remaining cream
mixture. Spoon into individual dishes. Chill until ready to serve. Garnish with
strips of orange zest and whipped cream.

Makes 6 servings

Zitronen Crème

3 egg yolks (see Note)
1 cup sugar
1 envelope unflavored gelatin
1/2 cup cold water
Juice of 2 lemons

Juice of 1 small orange
1 teaspoon grated lemon zest
1 teaspoon grated orange zest
3 egg whites
1 cup whipping cream

Beat the egg yolks with the sugar in a bowl with an electric mixer until thick. Mix the gelatin with the cold water in a large bowl. Microwave the gelatin for 30 to 60 seconds and stir. The gelatin must be clear. Stir a small amount of the hot gelatin into the egg mixture; stir the egg mixture into the gelatin. Add the lemon juice, orange juice, lemon zest and orange zest. Mix well and chill until the mixture begins to thicken.

Beat the cream in a bowl with an electric mixer until stiff peaks form. Beat the egg whites in a bowl with a mixer until stiff peaks form. Fold the whipped cream into the lemon mixture; then fold in the egg whites. Place the mixture in a serving bowl and chill until set.

Note: To avoid raw eggs that may carry salmonella, we suggest using an equivalent amount of pasteurized egg substitute and powdered egg whites.

Makes 6 servings

Warm Apple Crisp

1 cup sugar
1/8 teaspoon each cinnamon and salt
8 cups chopped peeled apples
   (about 12)
1 cup quick-cooking oats
1 cup packed brown sugar

1/4 teaspoon baking soda
1/4 teaspoon baking powder
1/2 cup (1 stick) butter
1/2 cup flour
1/4 teaspoon salt
Vanilla ice cream

Combine the sugar, cinnamon and 1/8 teaspoon salt in a bowl. Mix in the apples. Spoon into a greased 9x12-inch baking dish. Combine the oats, brown sugar, baking soda, baking powder, butter, flour and 1/4 teaspoon salt in a large bowl and mix until crumbly. Sprinkle the brown sugar mixture over the apples and pat down lightly. Bake at 350 degrees for 45 to 60 minutes. Serve warm with vanilla ice cream.

Makes 8 servings

Apples are Michigan's largest crop, enticing many to farm markets throughout the state. More Michigan festivals are organized around apples than any other theme. Hardly any metropolitan area in the state is far from an apple orchard.

Hot Cranberry Glögg

12 whole cloves
6 (3-inch) cinnamon sticks
12 cups cranberry juice
4 cups orange juice

1 cup lemon juice
1/2 cup sugar
1 tablespoon grated orange zest

Tie the cloves and cinnamon sticks in a piece of cheesecloth. Place the cheesecloth in a stockpot. Add the cranberry juice, orange juice, lemon juice, sugar and orange zest. Bring the mixture to a boil. Reduce the heat and simmer 5 minutes. Discard the spice bag. Serve the glögg in mugs.

Makes about 12 servings

Hot Mulled Michigan Cider

1 gallon Michigan apple cider
1/2 cup packed brown sugar
4 cinnamon sticks
1/2 teaspoon salt

1 tablespoon whole cloves
1 tablespoon whole allspice
Cinnamon sticks

Combine the apple cider, brown sugar and 4 cinnamon sticks in a stockpot. Tie the salt, cloves and allspice in a small cheesecloth bag. Add the bag to the cider mixture. Heat the cider and simmer about 20 minutes. Discard the spice bag. Serve the hot cider in mugs with cinnamon sticks for stirring.

Makes about 16 servings

Wassail

1 (750-milliliter) bottle spiced rum
1 gallon each water and apple juice
Southern Comfort to taste

1 orange, sliced
6 whole cloves
Cinnamon sticks

Simmer the rum, water, apple juice, Southern Comfort, orange slices, cloves and cinnamon sticks in a large Dutch oven or stockpot until hot. Remove and discard the cloves and cinnamon sticks.

Makes about 36 servings

FROM OUR LOCAL CHEFS

Colin Brown
TOWNSEND HOTEL

Tanya Fallon
FORTÉ

Keith Famie

Greg Goodman
CAFÉ BON HOMME

Paul Grosz
CUISINE RESTAURANT

Tim Gzinsky
OPUS ONE

Rick Halberg
EMILY'S RESTAURANT

THE LARK

Giovanni Jack Leone

Dave Lumsden

MGM GRAND CASINO

Jimmy Schmidt
THE RATTLESNAKE CLUB

Michael Trombley
THE GOLDEN MUSHROOM

Takashi Yagihashi
TRIBUTE

Margo Yopek
OCEAN GRILLE

Maryland Crab Cakes with Key Lime Aïoli

2 tablespoons lemon juice
1 egg, beaten
6 tablespoons bread crumbs
1 1/2 teaspoons Worcestershire sauce
1/4 cup flour
1/4 cup mayonnaise

2 tablespoons English mustard
Salt and pepper to taste
1 pound jumbo lump crab meat
Butter
Key Lime Aïoli (below)

Combine the lemon juice, egg, bread crumbs, Worcestershire sauce, flour, mayonnaise and mustard. Season with salt and pepper and mix well. Gently fold in the crab meat. Shape into 2-ounce cakes. Melt enough butter to just coat the bottom of a large skillet. Add the crab cakes and sauté on each side until golden brown. Serve the crab cakes with Key Lime Aïoli.

Makes 4 servings

Key Lime Aïoli

1/2 cup egg yolks (see Note)
3/4 cup olive oil
5 tablespoons Key lime juice
1 tablespoon white vinegar
1/2 teaspoon minced garlic

1 tablespoon chopped fresh thyme
1 tablespoon sugar
Salt and pepper to taste
1 cup mayonnaise

Place the egg yolks in a bowl. Gradually add the olive oil, whisking constantly until the egg yolks thicken. Gradually add the Key lime juice, vinegar, garlic, thyme and sugar. Season with salt and pepper. Stir in the mayonnaise.

Note: To avoid raw eggs that may carry salmonella, we suggest using an equivalent amount of pasteurized egg substitute.

Makes about 2 cups

Chef Colin Brown, Townsend Hotel
Birmingham, Michigan

Lobster Ravioli

4 ounces sea scallops
4 ounces uncooked lobster meat
1 teaspoon tomato paste
1 egg white
Salt and pepper to taste
1/4 cup heavy cream
1 egg
Pasta sheets or won ton wrappers
4 ounces cooked lobster meat, sliced
Lobster sauce or flavored butter sauce

Place the sea scallops, uncooked lobster, tomato paste and egg white in a food processor. Season with salt and pepper. Purée the mixture. Add the heavy cream and purée again until the mixture thickens.

Beat the egg with a small amount of water in a cup. Spread pasta sheets on a work surface. Place 1 ounce of the scallop mixture and 1 lobster slice on a pasta sheet. Brush the pasta sheet with the egg mixture. Cover the filling with a second pasta sheet and press the edges to seal. Cut out ravioli with a round cutter. Repeat with the remaining filling.

Bring a large saucepan of salted water to a boil. Add the ravioli and boil for 7 minutes. Drain well. Serve the ravioli with lobster sauce.

Makes 4 servings

Chef Paul Grosz, Cuisine Restaurant
Detroit, Michigan

Opus One Shrimp Hélène

Shrimp

16 jumbo shrimp
1 tablespoon minced garlic
Juice of 1/2 lemon
3/4 teaspoon salt

1/8 teaspoon white pepper, or to taste
1 (1-pound) box phyllo dough
1 cup clarified butter

Béarnaise Sauce

1 teaspoon melted butter
1 tablespoon minced shallots or onions
1/2 cup tarragon vinegar
1/2 teaspoon salt
2 tablespoons dried tarragon
1/8 teaspoon cayenne pepper

4 egg yolks
2 tablespoons water
2 cups warm clarified butter
Juice of 1/2 lemon
Salt and pepper to taste

For the shrimp, peel and devein the shrimp, leaving the tails on. Place the shrimp in a stainless steel bowl or nonreactive dish. Add the garlic, lemon juice, salt and pepper and marinate for 10 to 15 minutes. Lay 1 sheet of phyllo dough on a large cutting board or work table. Brush lightly with the clarified butter, starting at the edges and working toward the center. Place a second sheet of phyllo directly on top of the first sheet. Brush with butter in the same way. Keep the remaining phyllo sheets covered with a slightly damp towel to prevent the phyllo from drying out. Cut the buttered phyllo dough lengthwise into 4 equal strips. Place 1 marinated shrimp on the end of 1 of the phyllo strips. Roll up, covering all but the shrimp tail. Repeat the process until all the shrimp are wrapped in phyllo. Keep the shrimp covered with plastic wrap and refrigerated until ready to bake. Place a wire roasting rack in a roasting pan and place the shrimp on the wire rack (or directly on a baking sheet). Bake at 400 degrees 10 to 15 minutes, or until golden brown.

For the sauce, place the melted butter in a small nonreactive sauté pan. Add the shallots and sauté briefly. Add the vinegar, salt, tarragon and cayenne pepper. Cook to reduce the vinegar mixture until approximately 1 tablespoon of liquid remains. Remove the vinegar mixture from the heat and cool to room temperature. Place the egg yolks in a stainless steel bowl. Add the water and whisk with the egg yolks. Place the egg yolk mixture in the top of a double boiler. Add the tarragon vinegar reduction and whisk constantly until the egg yolks double in volume. Remove from the heat and whisk in the clarified butter. Add the lemon juice and season with salt and pepper. Keep warm until ready to serve.

Makes 16 servings

Chef Tim Gzinsky, Opus One
Detroit, Michigan

Chicken and Tart Cherry Won Tons

Won Tons

1 green bell pepper
1 red bell pepper
1 bunch scallions
1 cup dried cherries
1 boneless skinless chicken breast
Salt and pepper to taste

2 tablespoons sesame oil
1 egg
1 cup milk
1 package won ton wrappers
Vegetable oil for deep-frying

Secret Sauce (optional)

Orange marmalade
White horseradish

For the won tons, finely dice the bell peppers and scallions. Cut the cherries into small pieces. Trim the chicken of all fat and roast for 15 to 20 minutes, or until cooked through. Refrigerate the chicken until it is cool enough to handle. Chop the chicken into very small pieces. Combine the bell peppers, scallions, cherries and chicken in a bowl and mix well. Season with salt and pepper. Heat the sesame oil to 350 to 370 degrees in a medium sauté pan. Add the chicken mixture and sauté 2 to 3 minutes to blend the flavors. Remove the chicken from the heat and cool. Combine the egg and milk in a bowl and beat until smooth.

Lay a won ton wrapper on a work surface and place 1 tablespoon of the chicken mixture in the center. Dip a finger in the egg mixture and brush on two adjacent edges of the won ton wrapper. Fold the wrapper into a triangle and press the edges to seal. Bring 2 points of the triangle together and seal with a small amount of the egg mixture. Stuff and fold all won ton wrappers.

Heat vegetable oil for deep-frying in a large saucepan. Add a few won tons at a time to the oil and fry for 30 to 50 seconds, or until the won tons are light brown. Remove the won tons and drain on a tray covered with paper towels. Instead of being deep-fried, the won tons can be placed on a baking sheet and baked at 350 degrees for 10 to 15 minutes, or until browned.

For the sauce, blend 2 parts marmalade with 1 part horseradish in a bowl. Serve with the won tons.

Makes about 8 servings

Chef Dave Lumsden
Royal Oak, Michigan

Baked Brie in Phyllo Cups

1 (8-ounce) wheel Brie cheese
3 sheets phyllo dough
1/2 cup (1 stick) unsalted butter,
  melted

Hot pepper jelly or any sweet or savory
  jelly or jam

Cut the Brie cheese into 1/2-inch pieces. Place 1 sheet of phyllo dough on a flat dry surface. Brush the dough surface with melted butter. Place a second sheet of phyllo dough over the first, taking care to cover the entire surface. Brush with butter. Add 1 more sheet, but do not brush with butter. Cut the dough into 2-inch squares. Lightly spray miniature muffin cups with nonstick cooking spray. Arrange the phyllo dough squares over the cups. Press the dough into the cups, being careful not to tear the dough. Bake at 325 degrees for 7 to 10 minutes, or until lightly browned. Remove from the oven and cool. Place one piece of Brie in each cup and return to the oven just long enough to slightly melt the cheese. Carefully lift the cheese cups from the muffin cups and place on a serving platter. Top each with a drop of jelly. Serve immediately.

Makes 36 cups

Chef Dave Lumsden
Royal Oak, Michigan

Smoked Salmon and Boursin Pinwheels

1 wheel Boursin cheese, softened
1/2 cup heavy cream
1/2 pound sliced smoked salmon

4 to 5 sprigs fresh dillweed
Mild crackers or toast points

Blend the Boursin cheese with the cream in a bowl. Place slices of smoked salmon on a piece of plastic wrap. Spread the Boursin cheese mixture evenly over the salmon and sprinkle with dillweed. Carefully roll the salmon around the cheese to form a log. Place the log in the freezer for 20 to 30 minutes. Remove the log and slice into pinwheels. Serve with mild-flavored crackers or toast points.

Makes 36 pinwheels

Chef Dave Lumsden
Royal Oak, Michigan

Lobster Rockefeller Hors d'Oeuvre

4 slices bacon, cut into small pieces
1 Spanish onion, finely chopped
2 tablespoons chopped garlic
1 (10-ounce) package frozen chopped
   spinach, thawed
1 cup heavy cream
2 cups (8 ounces) grated Parmesan
   cheese

2 tablespoons Pernod (optional)
Salt and pepper to taste
1 (1-pound) box phyllo dough
1/2 cup (1 stick) unsalted butter,
   melted
2 cups cooked lobster meat, or
   1 package imitation lobster meat
1/2 teaspoon lemon juice

Place the bacon pieces in a heated medium saucepan and cook until the bacon
is crisp and the fat is rendered. Add the onion to the saucepan and cook until
translucent. Add the garlic and sauté lightly. Add the spinach and cook slightly.
Add the cream and bring to a boil. Reduce the heat and simmer until the cream is
reduced by half. Stir in the cheese and simmer until the mixture is thickened but
still a bit runny. Stir in the Pernod and season with salt and pepper. Remove from
the heat. Pour the spinach mixture onto a lightly greased baking sheet and
refrigerate until cool.

Unroll the phyllo dough and remove 1 sheet. Place it on a dry surface. Cover the
remainder with a damp towel so the phyllo doesn't dry out. Brush the phyllo sheet
with melted butter. Top with a second sheet of phyllo dough, covering the first one
completely. Brush the sheet with butter. Using a very sharp knife, cut the phyllo
dough into 2-inch-wide strips. Place about 1 tablespoon of the spinach mixture
at 1 corner end of each strip. Top with a 1-inch cube of lobster. Fold the open
corner end of the phyllo dough over the filling to form a triangle. Continue
folding into triangles like a flag until the entire strip is folded. Repeat with the
remaining filling. Place the triangles on a baking sheet and bake at 325 degrees
for 10 minutes, or until golden brown.

For a shortcut, spread a large amount of the spinach filling along the phyllo
strip and top with small pieces of lobster meat. Roll the phyllo into a log shape
and bake. Cut with a sharp serrated knife and serve. This is also delicious without
the lobster.

Makes about 12 servings

Chef Dave Lumsden
Royal Oak, Michigan

Rack of Lamb with Caramelized Pears and Chestnuts

2 racks of lamb, about 8 to 9 bones
   each, trimmed of the fat covering
   and the bones "Frenched" or
   trimmed to the meat loin
Sea salt to taste
Freshly ground pepper to taste
Extra-virgin olive oil
1 tablespoon chopped fresh rosemary
2 cups light vegetable, poultry or lamb
   stock

4 cups dry red wine
1/2 pound chestnuts, peeled
2 tablespoons unsalted butter
3 red Anjou pears, quartered
   lengthwise
2 tablespoons sugar
1 cup heavy cream
1 tablespoon chopped fresh rosemary
2 tablespoons unsalted butter
4 sprigs fresh rosemary

Take a large can about 5 to 6 inches in diameter, and place it in the center of a rack in a roasting pan. Arch the two racks of lamb, meat side out, around the can until the ends of the two racks touch each other. Wrap butcher's twine neatly around the racks just at the meat line to secure the meat in the "crown" circular shape. Remove the can carefully so the lamb stays securely in place. Season the lamb with salt and pepper. Drizzle a couple of drops of olive oil on the lamb and rub evenly and lightly across the surface so spices adhere. Sprinkle 1 tablespoon rosemary over the lamb.

Place the roasting pan on a rack in the center of the oven. Bake at 400 degrees about 10 minutes to sear. Continue cooking at 400 degrees for rare and medium-rare or turn down the temperature to 350 if you prefer your lamb medium or well-done. Test the roast with a small instant-read meat thermometer to detect your preferred degree of doneness after about 25 to 35 minutes, depending on the size of your lamb. Remove and allow to rest in a warm spot. Combine the stock and wine in a large skillet. Bring to a boil over high heat and cook until reduced and thick enough to coat the back of a spoon, about 15 minutes. Remove the lamb from the heat. Meanwhile, bring a medium saucepan of water to a simmer over medium-high heat. Add the chestnuts and cook about 15 minutes, or until tender. Drain. Break or cut the chestnuts in half.

Heat 2 tablespoons butter in a large nonstick skillet over high heat. Add the pears without crowding. Cook about 4 minutes to sear and brown their edges. Sprinkle the pears with sugar and turn the slices over. Add the chestnuts to lightly brown with the pears. Add the cream and 1 tablespoon rosemary and cook until the liquid is reduced and thick enough to coat the pears and chestnuts, about 5 minutes. Season with salt and pepper. Keep warm.

To serve, return the red wine sauce to the heat and bring to a simmer over medium-high heat. Whisk in 2 tablespoons butter. Season with salt and pepper. Remove from the heat and transfer to a serving boat.

Return the lamb to the oven to heat, about 5 minutes. Carefully transfer crown roast to the center of a serving platter, using two metal spatulas to lift the roast. Place a small can in the center of the roast. Top with a small bowl. Spoon the caramelized pears and chestnuts into the bowl. Stick the sprigs of rosemary into the center of the crown for garnish. Serve with the wine sauce on the side.

Makes 4 generous servings

Chef Jimmy Schmidt, The Rattlesnake Club
Detroit, Michigan

Miniature Beef Wellingtons

1/2 pound beef tenderloin
2 tablespoons chopped garlic
Salt and pepper to taste
2 cups mushrooms
1 large shallot

3 sprigs fresh thyme
1 egg
1 cup milk
1 (17-ounce) package puff pastry, thawed

Rub the beef tenderloin with garlic, salt and pepper. Roast the beef at 350 degrees until a meat thermometer reads 120 to 130 degrees. Remove the beef and refrigerate immediately. Finely chop the mushrooms and shallots; if using a food processor, be careful not to overprocess the mushrooms. Melt the butter in a medium sauté pan. Add the mushrooms, shallot and thyme to the pan and sauté until dry. Remove the vegetables from the heat and refrigerate. Cut the tenderloin into 1-inch square pieces. Combine the egg and milk in a bowl and beat until smooth. Remove 1 sheet of puff pastry and lay on a flat surface. Brush the top of the pastry with some of the egg mixture. Place the tenderloin pieces on the pastry about 1 inch apart. Top each piece of meat with 1 tablespoon of the mushroom mixture. Lay a second sheet of pastry on top of the first and form around the meat pieces. Cut out the pieces and press the edges of the pastry together to seal. Place the miniature beef Wellingtons on a lightly greased baking sheet and brush the tops with some of the egg mixture. Bake at 350 degrees for 10 to 15 minutes, or until puffed and browned.

Makes 6 servings

Chef Dave Lumsden
Royal Oak, Michigan

Poached Maine Lobster with Oxtail Risotto

3 (1 1/2-pound) live Maine lobster
Red Wine Braised Oxtail (below)
Red Wine Braised Oxtail Sauce
   (page 215)

Oxtail Risotto (page 215)
3 cups clarified butter
1 cup baby chervil sprouts
1 tablespoon chive oil

Cook the lobster in boiling water in a large stockpot for 5 minutes. Drain and place the lobster in an ice bath to chill. Drain again. Remove the meat from the lobster tail, claws and knuckles and refrigerate.

Heat the clarified butter in a saucepan over low heat. Add the lobster meat and cook for 3 minutes, slightly undercooking it.

To assemble the dish, place the risotto in a large bowl in the center of a plate. Add the oxtail, then the lobster. Sprinkle on chervil sprouts. Drizzle the chive oil around the plate. Spoon the oxtail sauce over the lobster.

Makes 6 servings

Red Wine Braised Oxtail

1 oxtail, cut into 6- to 8-inch lengths
Salt and pepper to taste
2 tablespoons flour
1 cup olive oil
1 onion, diced
6 garlic cloves
1 celery rib, diced

1 carrot, diced
1 bottle dry red wine
2 cups veal stock
3 bay leaves
3 sprigs fresh thyme
1/2 cup honey (optional)

Season the oxtail with salt and pepper and dredge the pieces in flour. Heat the olive oil in a roasting pan. Add the oxtail and sear until golden brown. Add the onion, garlic, celery and carrot and sauté 3 to 5 minutes. Add the red wine and continue to cook 10 minutes. Add the veal stock, bay leaves and thyme. Cover the roasting pan with heavy-duty aluminum foil. Roast at 375 degrees for 2 hours, or until the meat is tender. Season with salt and pepper. Add the honey if necessary for sweetness. Reserve the meat for the lobster dish and the braising liquid for the sauce.

Red Wine Braised Oxtail Sauce

Braising liquid from Red Wine Braised Oxtail
Salt and pepper to taste
1 teaspoon honey, or to taste

Pour the braising liquid into a large saucepan. Bring to a boil and skim off any foam on the top. Reduce the liquid by half. Season with salt and pepper. Strain the liquid through a fine mesh sieve. Sweeten with honey.

Oxtail Risotto

5 cups chicken stock
1 tablespoon butter
1 tablespoon olive oil
1 tablespoon minced onion
1 tablespoon minced mushrooms
1 tablespoon minced leeks
1 teaspoon minced garlic
$1^1/2$ cups arborio rice
$1/4$ cup dry white wine
2 tablespoons grated Parmesan cheese
Salt and pepper to taste

Bring the chicken stock to a boil in a stockpot. Reduce the heat to low and simmer. Melt the butter with the olive oil in a medium saucepan over medium heat. Add the onion, mushrooms, leeks and garlic and cook for 2 minutes. Add the rice and cook, stirring, 3 minutes, or until well coated with butter and oil. Add the wine and cook about 2 minutes, or until it evaporates. Gradually stir in 1 cup chicken stock. Let it almost evaporate; then add the remaining stock $1/2$ cup at a time. Add more stock and stir every 10 minutes, or as the liquid evaporates. When the rice is tender but slightly firm in the center, add the cheese and season with salt and pepper.

Executive Chef Takashi Yagihashi, Tribute
Farmington Hills, Michigan

Curried Duck Salad

1 cup good-quality mayonnaise
2/3 cup chutney, puréed
8 teaspoons good-quality curry powder
2 1/2 teaspoons fresh lemon juice
8 teaspoons honey
1 teaspoon white vinegar
Diced meat from 2 roast ducks

2 large celery ribs, peeled and finely
    chopped
1 small onion, finely chopped
2 apples, diced
1/4 cup sliced almonds, toasted
Salt and pepper to taste

Combine the mayonnaise, chutney, curry powder, lemon juice, honey and vinegar
in a large mixing bowl. Blend well. Add the duck, celery, onion, apples and almonds.
Toss well. Season with salt and pepper. Refrigerate at least 2 hours before serving.

Makes 8 appetizer servings

The Lark
West Bloomfield, Michigan

Salt-Baked Shrimp

20 shrimp, peeled and deveined
1 cup cornstarch
Vegetable oil for deep-frying

1 jalapeño chile, sliced
Salt to taste

Place the shrimp in a stockpot of boiling water and cook 2 minutes. Drain the
shrimp, but do not completely dry. Coat the shrimp with cornstarch. Heat the
vegetable oil to 400 degrees in a deep-fryer. Add the shrimp and cook 3 to
4 minutes or until done. Place a skillet on the stove and heat until it is very hot.
Add the jalapeño and shrimp and season with salt. Toss the chile and shrimp in
the skillet for 1 minute.

Makes 4 to 6 servings

The Lark
West Bloomfield, Michigan

Rack of Lamb Genghis Khan

3 (8-rib) racks of lamb, trimmed and silver skin removed
Lamb Marinade (below)
1 cup hoisin sauce

Place the lamb and the marinade in a plastic bag. Tie and refrigerate for 48 hours, turning occasionally. Remove the lamb from the marinade and let stand at room temperature for 1 hour before cooking. Brush the lamb with hoisin sauce. Place the lamb on a rack in a shallow roasting pan and roast at 450 degrees for 15 to 25 minutes for rare lamb, depending on the size of the racks, or longer for a greater degree of doneness. Let stand for 6 or 7 minutes before carving.

Makes 6 servings

Lamb Marinade

1 cup finely chopped onion
2 tablespoons minced garlic
3 tablespoons lemon juice
1/2 cup honey
3 tablespoons curry powder
1 1/2 teaspoons cayenne pepper
2 teaspoons dry mustard
2 teaspoons black pepper
2 tablespoons salt
1 cup water

Place the onion, garlic, lemon juice, honey, curry powder, cayenne pepper, dry mustard, black pepper, salt and water in a bowl and stir well to mix.

Makes about 2 1/2 cups

The Lark
West Bloomfield, Michigan

Pan-Crisped Wild Striped Bass

6 (6- to 7-ounce) striped bass fillets
Sea salt and freshly ground pepper to
   taste
Olive oil

Favorite mashed potatoes
Fresh snipped chives
Pipérade (below)

Trim the bass fillets to even squared-off pieces. Score the skin sides of the fish to prevent the fish from curling during the crisping. Season both sides of the fish with sea salt and pepper, seasoning the skin sides a bit more generously.

Heat a small amount of olive oil almost to smoking in 1 or 2 heavy-bottomed skillets. Carefully place the seasoned fillets, skin-side down, in the skillet without crowding the fish. Cover the skillet with a lid. Reduce the heat to medium and pan-fry the fish, undisturbed, for 5 to 7 minutes. Remove the lid and check the fish for doneness. Serve the fish crispy skin up on a mound of mashed potatoes flavored with lots of chives and a scoop of the pipérade. This dish is also nice with a fresh herb and lemon vinaigrette served on the side.

Makes 6 servings

Pipérade

1 tablespoon (or more) extra-virgin
   olive oil
1 onion, sliced
1 red bell pepper, cored and diced
1 green bell pepper, cored and diced
1 yellow bell pepper, cored and diced
6 Roma tomatoes, peeled, seeded and
   chopped

2 teaspoons chopped fresh basil
2 teaspoons chopped fresh mint
2 teaspoons chopped fresh oregano
Salt and black pepper to taste
1/8 teaspoon crushed red pepper flakes,
   or 1 to 2 drops of Tabasco sauce

Heat the olive oil in a large skillet over medium heat. Add the onion and cook 3 to 4 minutes. Add the bell peppers, tomatoes, basil, mint and oregano. Cook down until most of the liquid is absorbed. Season with salt, black pepper and red pepper flakes.

Chef Rick Halberg, Emily's Restaurant
Northville, Michigan

Salade Niçoise

1 pound fresh green beans
Salt
2¹/2 cups cooked quartered unpeeled
   red-skin potatoes
1 large cucumber, peeled, seeded and
   sliced
¹/2 large red onion, quartered and
   thinly sliced
Dijon Vinaigrette (below)

Favorite salad greens
40 kalamata olives
8 hard-cooked eggs, quartered
16 tomato wedges
¹/2 cup capers
8 (4-ounce) tuna steaks, grilled
16 anchovies (optional)
Fresh basil, cut in julienne strips

Blanch the green beans in a stockpot of boiling salted water for 5 minutes. Drain
the green beans and refrigerate. Place the cold green beans, potatoes, cucumber and
red onion in a bowl. Pour in the Dijon Vinaigrette and mix thoroughly. Marinate
the vegetables 4 to 8 hours in the refrigerator. Place a small bed of salad greens on
a large plate. Mound a cup or so of marinated vegetables on the greens, drizzling
some of the dressing onto the greens. Arrange the olives, eggs, tomato wedges
and capers around the edge of the salad. Top with a warm tuna steak. Cross
2 anchovy fillets on the tuna and top with a sprinkling of basil. Repeat with the
remaining ingredients.

Makes 8 dinner-size salads

Dijon Vinaigrette

2 cups corn oil or vegetable oil
1 cup red wine vinegar
1¹/2 teaspoons kosher salt
Freshly ground pepper to taste
1 teaspoon basil
2 to 3 drops of Tabasco sauce

1 teaspoon Worcestershire sauce
³/4 cup sugar
6 tablespoons Honeycup mustard
1 cup ice cubes
¹/4 cup Dijon mustard

Mix the corn oil, vinegar, salt, pepper, basil, Tabasco sauce, Worcestershire sauce,
sugar and Honeycup mustard in a bowl. Add the ice and beat with an electric mixer
at low speed until the ice is melted. Add the Dijon mustard and mix until thickened.

Makes about 3¹/2 cups

Chef Margo Yopek, Ocean Grille
Birmingham, Michigan

Ocean Grille's Salmon Wellington

Wild Mushroom Ragout

2 tablespoons olive oil
1 tablespoon diced shallots
1 tablespoon minced garlic
1 pound mixed button, portobello and
    shiitake mushrooms, sliced

3 sun-dried tomatoes, halved
Salt and pepper to taste
1/4 cup sherry

Salmon Wellington

6 (4-ounce) center-cut pieces salmon

1 puff pastry sheet, thawed

Red Wine Sauce

1 bottle dry red wine
4 sprigs fresh thyme
1/2 cup chicken stock

1 tablespoon honey
1 tablespoon cornstarch (optional)
1/4 cup cold water (optional)

For the ragout, heat the olive oil in a large skillet. Add the shallots and garlic and sauté until soft. Add the mushrooms and sauté until all the liquid is gone and the mushrooms begin to brown. Add the sun-dried tomatoes and season with salt and pepper. Add the sherry, scraping up the browned bits from the bottom of the skillet. Refrigerate the mushroom mixture until cold. Finely chop the mushroom mixture with a knife, or pulse in a food processor.

To assemble the Wellingtons, remove the skin from the salmon. Sear the salmon to medium-rare doneness in a hot skillet. Cut the puff pastry into 6-inch squares. Place 1 ounce of the mushroom mixture in the center. Place the salmon, dark side up, on the mushroom mixture. Pull up the corners of the puff pastry to encase the salmon. Pinch the puff pastry edges to seal. Place the salmon seal side down on a baking sheet. Repeat with the remaining salmon. Bake at 400 degrees for 20 minutes, or until the pastry is golden brown.

For the sauce, place the wine and thyme in a heavy saucepan over high heat and reduce to 1/3 the volume. Add the chicken stock and cook on medium-high heat for 10 minutes. Add the honey and stir. For a thicker sauce, stir the cornstarch into the cold water. Add the cornstarch mixture gradually to the hot wine sauce and thicken to the desired consistency. To serve, arrange the salmon portions on pools of red wine sauce.

Makes 6 servings

Chef Margo Yopek, Ocean Grille
Birmingham, Michigan

Grilled Pork Loin, Bistro Style

5 pounds pork tenderloin
3 ounces honey
1/4 cup dry mustard

2 tablespoons curry powder
2 tablespoons ground cumin
1 teaspoon crushed pepper

Rub the pork tenderloin with honey. Mix the dry mustard, curry powder, cumin and pepper in a bowl. Rub the mustard mixture onto the pork tenderloin. Place on a tray and refrigerate 6 hours. Grill or sear the pork until brown. To finish, roast the pork at 400 degrees until cooked through.

Makes 6 to 8 servings

Chef Greg Goodman, Cafe Bon Homme
Plymouth, Michigan

Field Greens Salad

2 teaspoons chopped red onion
1 teaspoon Dijon mustard
2 tablespoons cherry balsamic vinegar
1 teaspoon chopped fresh tarragon
1/4 cup extra-virgin olive oil
Salt and pepper to taste

2 cups field greens
3 ounces chèvre cheese
1/4 cup pine nuts, toasted
3 tablespoons dried cherries
1/4 cup crispy julienne-cut carrots

Place the red onion, Dijon mustard, balsamic vinegar and tarragon in a mixing bowl. Gradually add the olive oil and stir to create an emulsion. Season with salt and pepper. Add the greens and toss with the vinaigrette. Place the salad on a plate. Top with the chèvre cheese, pine nuts, dried cherries and carrots.

Makes 2 servings

Chef Michael Trombley, The Golden Mushroom
Southfield, Michigan

Chestnut-Crusted Venison with Asian Flavors

1 (6-ounce) venison loin, cleaned of sinew
Salt and pepper to taste
1/8 teaspoon allspice, or to taste
2 tablespoons Dijon mustard
3 ounces roasted chestnuts, finely ground
1/4 cup sesame oil
1/4 cup sliced carrots
4 small bok choy, cut in quarters
6 slices lotus root
2 cups mixed braising greens
1/4 cup julienne-cut red bell pepper
1/4 cup julienne-cut yellow bell pepper
1 1/2 cups cooked seasoned sticky rice
1 tablespoon black sesame seeds, toasted
2 tablespoons fried julienne-cut gingerroot
2 tablespoons sesame ginger sauce
1 tablespoon veal demi-glace

Season the venison with salt, pepper and allspice. Brush the venison with the Dijon mustard and pat on the ground chestnuts. Heat a 12-inch sauté pan or skillet over high heat until hot. Reduce the heat to medium. Add half the sesame oil to the pan. Add the venison and sear on all sides. Remove the venison from the pan and place on a rack in a shallow roasting pan. Roast at 350 degrees until a meat thermometer registers 135 degrees and the meat is medium-rare. Remove the venison and keep warm.

Heat a large sauté pan until hot. Add the remaining sesame oil. Add the carrots, then the bok choy. Sauté 1 to 2 minutes. Add the lotus root, braising greens and red and yellow bell peppers. Sauté the vegetables until tender.

Slice the venison. Place the sticky rice on a serving platter. Add the vegetables and arrange the venison on the platter. Sprinkle with the sesame seeds and fried gingerroot. Drizzle with sesame ginger sauce and veal demi-glace.

Makes 2 servings

Chef Michael Trombley, The Golden Mushroom
Southfield, Michigan

Rabbit Risotto with Morel Mushrooms

Rabbit legs
Allspice, ground cloves and thyme
  to taste
Chopped onion
Salt to taste
Olive oil
Chicken stock (optional)
4 ounces rabbit loin, cleaned of sinew
Pepper to taste
2 tablespoons unsalted butter
1 teaspoon chopped shallots
1/2 cup fresh morel mushrooms

1/4 cup heavy cream
2 tablespoons unsalted butter
1 teaspoon chopped garlic
2 tablespoons julienne-cut sun-dried
  tomatoes
2 cups cooked risotto
1/2 cup dry white wine
1 cup low-sodium chicken stock
2 tablespoons grated Parmesan cheese
Chopped herbs to taste
1 tablespoon basil oil
1 teaspoon 20-year-old balsamic vinegar

For the confit, season the rabbit with allspice, cloves, thyme, onion and salt. Cover and refrigerate overnight. Rinse the rabbit and place in a heavy stockpot. Pour in enough olive oil to coat the rabbit. Cover the pan and bake at 250 degrees 4 hours, or until the rabbit is tender. Remove the meat from the bones. Heat a 12-inch sauté pan or skillet over high heat until hot. Season the rabbit loin with salt and pepper and add to the pan to sear. Reduce the heat and cook the rabbit until medium-rare. Remove from the pan and let stand. Thinly slice the meat. Heat a sauté pan until hot and add 2 tablespoons butter and the shallots. Cook the shallots until partially done. Add the mushrooms and cook until soft. Add the cream and cook until the liquid is reduced. Season with salt and pepper.

For the risotto, heat a 2-quart saucepan over high heat until hot. Add 2 tablespoons butter and the garlic. Cook until the garlic is tender. Add the sun-dried tomatoes and risotto. Add the white wine and chicken stock and stir constantly. When the rice mixture is hot, add the cheese and chopped herbs. Fold in the rabbit confit and place the risotto mixture on a serving plate. Add the sliced rabbit loin and drizzle basil oil and balsamic vinegar on the outer portion of the plate. Garnish the plate with the cream sauce.

Makes 2 servings

Chef Michael Trombley, The Golden Mushroom
Southfield, Michigan

Smoked Whitefish Won Tons with Ginger Sauce

Won Tons

8 ounces fresh pickerel or fresh
   whitefish, boned and cut into
   chunks
4 ounces smoked whitefish, boned and
   cut into chunks

Salt and pepper to taste
1 cup heavy cream
16 (6-inch-square) won ton wrappers

Ginger Soy Sauce

1/2 cup soy sauce
1/4 cup fresh orange juice
1 teaspoon grated gingerroot

1/4 cup rice wine vinegar
2 teaspoons chopped fresh cilantro

For the won tons, place the bowl of a food processor in the refrigerator at least 30 minutes to chill. Remove the cold bowl and fit it with a steel blade. Add the pickerel and smoked whitefish and season with salt and pepper. Pulse the fish mixture for 5 to 10 seconds. With the food processor on, gradually add the cream until the filling is firm but still soft. It should have a mousse-like consistency. Place about 2 tablespoons of the fish mixture in the center of each won ton wrapper. Encase the filling by bringing up the sides of the wrapper and pinching the edges together at the top to form sack-like bundles.

Place the filled won tons in a steamer basket over boiling water. Cover the steamer and cook 12 to 15 minutes, or until the filling is cooked. Work in batches if necessary. Remove the cooked won tons from the steamer and keep warm.

For the sauce, combine the soy sauce, orange juice, gingerroot and rice wine vinegar in a medium saucepan. Bring the mixture to a boil. Reduce the heat and stir in the cilantro.

To assemble, place the won tons on a serving plate and drizzle with the Ginger Soy Sauce. Serve immediately.

Makes 16 won tons

Chef Keith Famie
West Bloomfield, Michigan

Michigan Apple and Cherry Cobbler

3 cups (6 sticks) butter
1¹/2 cups packed brown sugar
2 cinnamon sticks
8 Granny Smith apples, peeled, cored and diced
1¹/2 cups dried Michigan cherries
¹/2 cup brandy
3 sheets pie pastry or puff pastry
1 egg
Whipped cream

Place the butter in a large sauté pan. Add the brown sugar and cinnamon sticks and cook until the butter and brown sugar melt together. Add the apples and cherries and mix in the brandy. Cook the fruit over medium heat 10 minutes, stirring occasionally, or until the apples are soft. Remove the fruit from the heat and cool to room temperature. If desired, do this step a day in advance and refrigerate the mixture.

Remove and discard the cinnamon sticks. Fill 4 ceramic dishes or 1 large glass or ceramic baking dish with the apple mixture. Cut the pie pastry into leaf shapes using a small paring knife. Arrange the leaves over the apple mixture, being sure to cover all the mixture with the leaves. Mix the egg with a small amount of water in a cup. Brush over the pastry leaves. Bake at 400 degrees for 15 to 20 minutes, or until the pastry is golden brown. Serve with whipped cream.

Makes 4 servings

Chef Keith Famie
West Bloomfield, Michigan

Simple but Deadly Chocolate Espresso Cake

1 cup (2 sticks) unsalted butter
1/2 cup double-strength brewed coffee or brewed espresso
2/3 cup packed light brown sugar
8 ounces good-quality semisweet chocolate, chopped
2 eggs
2 egg yolks
2 egg whites
Confectioners' sugar (optional)
Vanilla or coffee crème anglaise (optional)

Place the butter, coffee and brown sugar in a saucepan and heat until the brown sugar is completely dissolved. Bring the mixture to a soft boil. Remove from the heat and add the chopped chocolate. Stir the chocolate mixture until smooth. Cool to room temperature. Place the eggs and egg yolks in a stainless steel or glass bowl. Whisk the eggs well. Stir in the chocolate mixture. Whip the egg whites to stiff peaks in a bowl using an electric mixer. Gently fold the egg whites into the chocolate mixture, making sure not to overmix.

Spray a 5x9-inch loaf pan with nonstick cooking spray. Line the sides of the pan with parchment paper. Gently spoon the chocolate mixture into the loaf pan. Place the loaf pan in a larger baking pan. Add enough water to reach halfway up the sides of the loaf pan. Bake at 350 degrees for 60 to 70 minutes, depending on the whims of your oven. The cake will look under-baked when done. Remove the loaf pan from the water bath and refrigerate at least 12 to 24 hours. Invert the cake onto a serving platter and cut into slices. Serve plain; with a light dusting of confectioners' sugar; or with vanilla or coffee crème anglaise.

Makes 6 servings

Chef Giovanni Jack Leone

Brown Derby Grapefruit Cake

Cake

2 1/4 cups sifted cake flour
1 1/2 cups sugar
1 tablespoon baking powder
1 teaspoon salt
5 egg yolks
1/2 cup corn oil

3/4 cup cold water
Grated zest of 1 lemon
2 teaspoons vanilla extract
8 egg whites
1/2 teaspoon cream of tartar

Grapefruit Frosting

1 (2-pound) can grapefruit sections,
    well drained
24 ounces cream cheese, softened
4 teaspoons lemon juice

1 cup confectioners' sugar
12 drops of yellow food coloring
2 teaspoons grated lemon zest

For the cake, sift together the flour, sugar, baking powder and salt into a large mixing bowl. Add the egg yolks 1 at a time. Add the corn oil, water, lemon zest and vanilla and mix with a wooden spoon or handheld blender. Place the egg whites and cream of tartar in a large bowl and whip to stiff peaks with an electric mixer. Gently fold the egg whites into the egg yolk mixture just until blended. Do not stir. Pour the batter into two 10-inch round cake pans. Bake at 325 degrees for 55 minutes. Increase the oven temperature to 350 and bake an additional 10 minutes. The cake is done when the top springs back to the touch. Invert the layers onto a wire rack to cool.

For the frosting, mash 6 grapefruit sections into small bits with a fork; reserve the remaining grapefruit. Beat the cream cheese with the lemon juice in a large bowl with an electric mixer until fluffy. Gradually beat in the sugar. Add the food coloring, lemon zest and 4 teaspoons of the crushed grapefruit.

To assemble the cake, place 1 layer bottom-side up on a serving plate. Spread with the frosting and top with grapefruit sections. Cover with the second cake layer, bottom-side down. Frost the top and side of the cake. Garnish with the grapefruit sections.

Makes 12 servings

MGM Grand Casino
Detroit, Michigan

Chocolate Cream Pie

Chocolate Pie Pastry

1/2 cup (1 stick) unsalted butter, softened
1 cup confectioners' sugar

1 1/4 cups flour
1/4 cup baking cocoa, sifted
4 egg yolks

Chocolate Cream

1 cup milk
1 cup heavy cream
1 vanilla bean
3 egg yolks

1/4 cup sugar
6 ounces bittersweet chocolate, broken
   into pieces

Pastry Cream

1 cup milk
2 tablespoons unsalted butter
3 tablespoons sugar
1 vanilla bean, split
2 egg yolks

1 1/2 tablespoons cornstarch
2 teaspoons sugar
2 cups whipping cream
1 tablespoon Grand Marnier, or
   1 teaspoon vanilla extract

For the pie pastry, cream the butter and confectioners' sugar in a large bowl with an electric mixer until smooth. Add the flour and cocoa. Mix well, scraping the side of the bowl. The mixture will look mealy. Add the egg yolks 1 at a time, mixing well after each addition and scraping the side of the bowl. The dough will be quite sticky. Shape into a disk and place between 2 sheets of plastic wrap.

Roll out the dough to a 13-inch or larger circle. Fit the dough into a 12-inch tart pan with a removable bottom. Place a sheet of aluminum foil on top of the dough. Weigh down the foil with pie weights or dry beans. Bake at 350 degrees for 10 to 15 minutes, or until the dough is firm. Remove the crust from the oven and let cool. Remove the pie weights and the foil. Set the pastry aside.

For the chocolate cream, combine the milk, cream and vanilla bean in a medium saucepan. Bring the mixture to a boil. Whisk the egg yolks and sugar together in a bowl. Slowly pour about 1/2 cup of the hot cream mixture into the egg yolks, whisking constantly. Add the egg yolk mixture to the remaining hot cream mixture, stirring constantly with a wooden spoon, until the mixture is thick enough to coat the back of a spoon, about 5 minutes. Place the chocolate pieces in a bowl. Strain the hot cream mixture and slowly whisk the cream into the chocolate until the chocolate is melted and the mixture is smooth. Place the bowl over an ice bath to cool.

For the pastry cream, bring the milk, butter, 3 tablespoons sugar and the vanilla bean to a boil in a medium saucepan. Mix the egg yolks, cornstarch and 2 teaspoons sugar together in a bowl. Whisk a small amount of the hot milk mixture into the egg mixture. Then whisk the egg mixture back into the hot milk mixture. Whisk the egg mixture vigorously for 5 minutes, or until it is thick and just comes to a boil. Discard the vanilla bean and remove the mixture from the heat.

Pour the egg mixture into a food processor and process 30 seconds or until smooth. Pour the egg mixture into a shallow bowl. Cover with plastic wrap touching the cream to prevent a skin from forming. Refrigerate until cool.

Use 1 cup pastry cream for the Chocolate Cream Pie; the remaining 1 cup can be refrigerated for another recipe. Whip the whipping cream in a bowl with an electric mixer until stiff peaks form. Whisk 1 cup of pastry cream with the Grand Marnier in a bowl until smooth. Whisk the pastry cream and whipped cream together. Do not overwhisk.

To assemble, spread the chocolate mixture in the prepared tart shell. Top with the whipped cream mixture, using a pastry bag with a large star tip or smoothing on the whipped cream with a spatula.

Makes 12 servings

Head Pastry Chef Tanya Fallon, Forté
Birmingham, Michigan

CONTRIBUTORS

We would like to thank all of our friends, family, and members of the Junior League of Birmingham for the countless hours that they generously devoted to collecting recipes. We would like to express our deepest gratitude to those listed here and apologize to anyone whom we may have inadvertently failed to mention.

Karen Anderson
Peg Anderson
Carol Angelina
Amy Angell
Kathleen Angell
Cedric Ballarin
Jennifer Ballarin
Chef Bill Barum
Nancy Belanger
Annie Bergeron
Melanie Berry
Carol Berutti
Pam Berutti
Ruth Best
Pat Bishop
Susan Boese
Carol Borson
Keri Boyd
Rebecca Brehm
Chef Colin Brown
Kim Kley Brown
Nancy Burgess
Debbie Caiati
Jean Carabio
Karen Caserio
Susan Cavaretta
Victoria P. Cendrowski
Chef Marcey Clark
Robin Cook
Charlotte Coyne
Donna Coyne
Donna Craparotta
Jill Craparotta
Janet Cummins
Alice Currier
Dorothy Doran
Emily Ann Eberhart
Jane Emanoil
Charlene Ervin

Dennis Ervin
Cory Esterline
Jennifer Evans
Chef Tanya Fallon
Chef Keith Famie
Angie Ferryman
Shirley Franks
Patricia Frederick
Kim Frye
Kristen Gischia
Judy Gmeiner
Chef Greg Goodman
Laurie Greben
Lisa Gross
Chef Paul Grosz
Tracy Gyarfas
Chef Tim Gzinsky
Chef Rick Halberg
Andrea Hamer
Bonnie Hannigan
Barbara Hart
Lisa Healy
Dennis Hill
Mary Hunter
Tracy Jaffe
Kristen Jamison
Margaret John
Pam Johnson
Christy Kauffman
Julie Keesor
Carolyn Kerr
Ray Kethledge
Stacey Kipke
Jim Kirila
Cindy Koontz
Barbara Kruh
Sue Kwiatkowski
James Laird
Molly Lamarche

Ashley Lane
Liz Lee
Lynn Leipold
Chef Giovanni Jack
   Leone
Melissa Leupp
Marian Loomis
Chef Dave Lumsden
Lisa Lundquist
Dorothy Mabley
Sally Mager
Molly Markley
Lynn Martignon
Liz McClean
Donna McDonald
Mary McMurdo
Liz Meyer
Helene Mills
Gertrude Modjewski
Jamie Sue Morrison
Mary Margaret Mudge
Tom Mudge
Georgette Nader
Nancy Nagle
Beth Nelles
Colette O'Connor
Wendy Patterson
Dena Raminick
Katie Randlett
Bonnie Reed
Karen Reed
Anne Reeves
Gigi Rey
Linda Richards
Carrie Riker
Amy Risius
Bernadette Risius
Lisa Rivera
Daryl Robbins

Sandy Rogal
Mary Jo Rosen
Mary Ross
Michelle Royer
Barbara Ruth
Kelley Samberg
Chef Jimmy Schmidt
Kerry Schneeberger
Judy Schoelgel
Carol Schupbach
Louise Scott
Sally Scott
Shawn Scott
Fran Seleski
Elaine Shelton
Lynn Shelver
Steve Sloan
Carrie Sofikitis
Jennifer Soley
Virginia Soley
Shelly Stanick
Mary Stehney
Sandra Stehney
Leslie Tatum
Scott Thorpe
Sue Tomilson
Heather Toutant
Chef Michael Trombley
Sandy Ummel
Inge Vastola
Barbara Velasco
Billie Wald
Amy Wilcox
Jodi Wolfe
Chef Takashi Yagihashi
Chef Margo Yopek
Nanette Yuhasz

Once the recipes were collected, the testing process began. We would like to thank all of our friends, family, and League members who devoted the extensive time required to test each recipe. Their tireless efforts are reflected in the pages of this cookbook. We apologize to anyone whom we may have inadvertently failed to mention.

Karen Anderson
Laura Andoni
Amy Angell
Katie Baetz
Jennifer Ballarin
Marty Barrett
Melissa Barrett
Andrea Bartl
Lena Battle
Nancy Belanger
Annie Bergeron
Pam Berutti
Kim Biddinger
Jody Boughton
Keri Boyd
Karen Boyk
Rebecca Brehm
Jody Brennan
Karen Burr
Carolyn Canham
Jean Carabio
Laurie Chase
Pamela Cohen
Bridget Collins
Robin Cook
Andrea Craparotta
Julie Crowner
Janet Cummins
Wendy Cummins
Teena Dale
Darcy Davis
Renee Delsignore
Laura Dickerson
Jennifer Dix
Allison Donnelly
Debbie Dronsejko
Anne Leo Duffy
Elizabeth Eads
Emily Eberhart

Dana Elliott
Jennifer Evans
Sandra Farney
Melissa Miller Farr
Angie Ferryman
Kathy Fishburn
Elaine Fitzpatrick
Tricia Fitzsimons
Cathy Frost
Kristen Goran
Kathy Greenbury
Susan Hare
Katie Hart
Carolyn Harvey
Sonia Hassan
Jean Hastings
Lisa Healy
Kathy Hillstrom
Jill Hilty
Laurie Hinckley
Andrea Hofley
Laurie Horvath
Mary Hunter
Kristen Jamison
Carolyn Kerr
Corinne Kesteloot
Jessica Kethledge
Stacey Kipke
Debbie Klein
Laura Knipfer
Barb Kuczynski
Molly Lamarche
Ashley Lane
Mary Ligon
Kellee Linsley
Beth Luecke
Lisa Lundquist
Dorothy Mabley
Janet Madigan

Kathy Malone
Kim McGlynn
Jacki Mertz
Kelly Miller
Kerrie Montgomery
Patty Moore
Robin Moulton
Mary Margaret Mudge
Shelly Mulanax
Sara Mularoni
Alison Murphy
Nancy Nagle
Colette O'Connor
Kristen Parent
Laura Parker
Lisa Parker
Wendy Patterson
Kristen Pengelly
Julie Postma
Gigi Rey
Amy Risius
Bernadette Risius
Lisa Rivera
Kay Rollage
Diane Romano
Marianne Lauridsen
    Ross
Todd Rumpsa
Angie Schmucker
Shauna Schwarz
Sally Scott
Fran Seleski
Kerry Selinsky
Heide Sequeira
Lynn Shelver
Stacia Skoog
Carrie Sofikitis
Jennifer Soley
Tracey Szerlag

Ann Tarkington
Shalise Tempest
Mary Tilson
Inge Vastola
Barbara Velasco
Julie Vento
Pam Vermiglio
Krista Wagner
Maureen Wagner
Christy Walker
Alicia Washeleski
Lisa Whateley
Amanda Stone Yntema
Amy Zimmer

SPONSORS

Individual Sponsors

Truffle ($501 to $1,000)
Colette and Brian O'Connor   Amy and Jeff Risius

Chocolate Soufflé
($101 to $500)   Susan Brodsky   Stacia Skoog
Karen Anderson   Diane Dickelmann   Jennifer Soley
Nancy Belanger   Jessica Neeper

Crème Brûlée
($51 to $100)   Lisa Healy   Julie Quinn Pietrosante
Contessa Bannon   K. K. Heiwig   Katie Randlett
Kathleen Belanger   Jill Hilty   Dawn Rassel
Ginny Bennett   Amy Hochkammer   Anne Reeves
Christina Bergstrom   Laurie Horvath   Gayle Roberts
Melanie Berry   Barbara Hughes   Mrs. Patricia Robinson
Pamela Berutti   Margaret John   Linda Rodney
Keri Boyd   Linda Juracek-Lipa   Sandra and Ray Rogal
Gale Colwell   Pamela Kanehann   Mary Ross
Robin Cook   Leslie Kellett   Courtney Runco
Mary Lou Craig   Laura Ketko   Jane Ruzumna
Wendy and Patrick Cummins   Mollie Laethem   Molly Saeli
Alice Currier   Elizabeth Linck   Kelley Samberg
Teena Dale   Carolyn MacAdam   Suzanne Sanders
Karen DeKoker   Janet Madigan   Angie Schmucker
Renee Delsignore   Jennifer Margherio   Mrs. (Norma) Leigh Smith
Jennifer Dix   Krysta McNaughton   Michelle Stuhlreyer
Jennifer Evans   Jackie Mertz   Tracey Szerlag
Mary Feldman   JoAnne Meurer   Jennifer Taylor
Karin Flint   Michelle Moody   Suzanne Tosto
Jennifer Gardner   Anne Neidhart   Heather Ward
Peggy Geisler   Tricia Ong   Alicia Washeleski
Kathy Greenbury   Laura Parker   Ann Watts
Susan Griffin   Wendy Patterson
Karen Haeffner   Priscilla Perkins

Individual Sponsors (continued)

Meringue (up to $50)

Stacie Adkins
Jackie Alberti
Amy Angell
Jennifer Ballarin
Martha Barrett
Melissa Bingham
Martha Bones
Cathy Bridenstine
Michelle Clement
Bridget Collins
Karen Daniels
Allison Donnelly
Betty Emmert
Kristin Fettig
Cathy Frost
Kim Frye
Patty Ghesquiere

Nanette Grace
Frances Greenebaum
Khal Hanna
Sonia Hassan
Laurie Hinckley
Helene Holmes
Jill Houlihan
Cheryl Houpt
Corinne Kesteloot
Susan Krueger
Molly Lamarche
Elaine Lewenz
Courtney Lowman
Janet Mailley
Jill Maisano
Kathy Malone
Marion McDonnell

Jennifer Mills
Kerrie Montgomery
Mary Linda Murphy
Andrea Niemeyer
Jennifer Nystrom
Erin O'Brien
Christine O'Malley
Christine Parizeau
Nicole Philheart
Lynn Quigley
Meg Schulte
Melissa Swiecicki
Shelley Wagner
Whitney Wagner
Shannon Waid
Amanda Stone Yntema
Amy Zimmer

Corporate Sponsors

Nordstrom's
Tiffany & Co.

In-Kind Donors

Forté Restaurant
MGM Grand Hotel
Tuscan Express, Grand Rapids, Michigan

Publications
Michigan in Quotes
Tom Powers

Michigan's Capital Cities: From Asparagus to Stump Fences
Melissa Stimson and M. F. Chatfield
Thunder Bay Press
Copyright 1997

Organizations
Michigan Economic Development Corporation—Travel Michigan
Cherry Marketing Institute—Michigan

Landscape Photography
Travel Michigan (pages 10 and 18)
Randall McCune (page 14)
Gaylord/Otsego County CVB (page 22)

Artists
Our illustrations were done by Christina Schloss Forhan, who was employed as an information systems consultant until she dedicated herself to her vocation as mom to three great kids and wife. Now, she volunteers in the schools, community, and church. She illustrates for fun and lends her artistic talents to charitable organizations.

Virginia Hutchins has been a food stylist for twenty years. Her background includes formal training in graphic design and work as an art director for a regional department store chain in Ohio. She lives in Cleveland, Ohio, and travels all over the United States to work on national accounts for both still photography and television commercials. She really enjoys the food styling she does for regional cookbooks. She says, "The cookbook coordinators always work so hard to produce a superior book, and they give me the most interesting regional recipes to work on."

Jeff Hage has been a commercial photographer specializing in product, tabletop, and location shooting for more than fifteen years. He attended the Center for Creative Studies College of Art and Design in Detroit while working for several commercial studios. In 1989 he opened his first studio in downtown Detroit, moving to Hamtramck's artist community and then to the Royal Oak area. Upon relocating to western Michigan in 1996, Jeff honed his skills as a digital photographer for a medical equipment company and then returned to the freelance world. His unique sensitivity for light and composition provides award-winning imagery for his clients around the country and the world.

ORDER FORM

Name _____

Address _____

City _____ State _____ Zip _____

Telephone ( ) _____ Email Address _____

Ship To: (if different address)

Name _____

Address _____

City _____ State _____ Zip _____

Telephone ( ) _____

Method of Payment

[ ] Check payable to Junior League of Birmingham, Cookbook
[ ] VISA   [ ] MasterCard

Name (as appears on card) _____

Card Number _____ Expiration Date _____

Signature _____

	QUANTITY	AMOUNT DUE
Seasons in Thyme at $29.95 per book	_____	_____
Seasons in Thyme at $161.73 per case of six	_____	_____

Shipping and Handling

$4.00 for first book; $2.00 for each additional book **OR** $10.00 per case   _____

Subtotal   _____

Sales Tax (Michigan residents add 6% on Subtotal. No tax if mailing out of state.)   _____

TOTAL   _____

Mail Order Form to: Junior League of Birmingham, Michigan, Inc.
123 West Brown Street
Birmingham, Michigan 48009
Telephone: (248) 646-2613

Fax order Form to: (248) 646-9447
Send via Email to: JLBINC@HTDConnect.com

Photocopies will be accepted.